Ingersoll Ontario Book 2 in Colour Photos, Saving Our History One Photo at a Time

Photography
by Barbara Raué
©2019

Series Name: Cruising Ontario

Book 239: Ingersoll Book 2

Cover photo: 130 King Street East, Page 16

©All the photos in this book have been taken with my cameras. I own the rights to them.

Series Name: Cruising Ontario, Saving Our History One Photo at a Time in colour photos

Books Available in Alphabetical Order:
Aberfoyle, Acton, Ajax, Alton, Amherstburg, Ancaster, Arthur, Auburn, Aylmer, Ayr, Beaver Valley, Belfountain, Belgrave, Belleville, Bloomingdale, Blyth, Brantford, Brockville, Burford, Burlington, Caledon, Caledonia, Cambridge, Carlow, Cayuga, Chatsworth, Cheltenham, Clifford, Colborne, Collingwood, Conestogo, Delhi, Dorchester to Aylmer, Drayton, Drumbo, Dundas, Dunlop, Dunnville, Eden Mills, Elmira, Elora, Embro, Erin, Essex, Fergus, Fort Erie, Georgetown, Goderich, Grimsby, Guelph, Hagersville, Haldimand County, Hamilton, Hanover, Harriston, Hespeler, Ingersoll, Inglewood, Innerkip, Jarvis, Kingston, Kingsville, Kitchener, Lake Superior, Lincoln, Linwood, Listowel, London, Lucknow, Merrickville, Mono, Mount Brydges, Mount Forest, Mount Pleasant, Neustadt, New Hamburg, Newboro, Newport, Niagara-on-the-Lake, Niagara Falls, North Bay, Oakville, Onondaga, Orangeville, Orillia, Oshawa, Otterville, Owen Sound, Palmerston, Paris, Parry Sound, Pelham, Perth, Peterborough, Petrolia, Pickering, Port Colborne, Port Elgin, Port Hope, Port Perry, Portland, Preston, Rockwood, Sarnia, Sault Ste. Marie, Seaforth, Sheffield, Shelburne, Simcoe, Smiths Falls, Smithville, Southampton, St. Catharines, St. George, St. Jacobs, St. Marys, St. Thomas, Stoney Creek, Stouffville, Stratford, Strathroy, Sudbury, Tavistock, Terra Cotta, Thamesford, Thunder Bay, Tillsonburg, Toronto, Uxbridge, Waterdown, Waterford, Waterloo, Welland, Wellesley, West Flamborough, Westport, Whitby, Windsor, Wingham, Woodstock, York

Book 236: Strathroy
Book 237: East Zorra
Book 238-239: Ingersoll

Table of Contents

King Street West	Page 5
King Street East	Page 13
Ingersoll Cheese Factory Museum	Page 19
Duke Street	Page 57
Hall Street	Page 59
Church Street	Page 59
Canterbury Street	Page 62
Victoria Street	Page 64
Ann Street	Page 65

The town of Ingersoll is ten miles from Woodstock, twenty-one miles from London, and ninety-eight from Toronto. Ingersoll was incorporated in 1865, and by the enterprise of its inhabitants enjoyed a steady and progressive growth. Most of the town was built on the sides and summit of the high gravelly banks of the River Thames, which flows through it and supplies constant water power, of which due advantage was taken by several factories at the waterside. The town got its name from a pioneer family named Ingersoll, who were among the first settlers in this district and took a very prominent part in the early career of the community.

It was situated on the Great Western Division of the Grand Trunk Railway, and also on the Credit Valley Branch of the Canadian Pacific. The country around is fertile, and large quantities of cheese were shipped from here. The manufacture of flour and cornmeal, with woolen and planing mills, a tannery and four agricultural implement factories, formed its chief industries; grain, livestock, and general manufactured products, in addition to cheese, formed its chief shipments.

In 1886 a special effort was made to induce desirable factories to locate here and in the following year the John Morrow Machine Screw Works, the Evans Bros. and Littler Piano factory and the Hault furniture factory were secured by giving liberal bonuses. Later on, the St. Charles Condenser and the Ingersoll Nut Factory were opened.

Ingersoll was the first town in Canada to adopt the silica-barytic sidewalks in 1890 when a contract was given to Otto Guelich of Detroit, to construct a sidewalk on the east side of Thames Street from the Atlantic House to the Baptist Tabernacle, a distance of three blocks. In 1891 a local company was organized with Walter Mills as manager, and year by year the work has been carried on till now nearly every street on both sides has a nice, clean, smooth silica-barytic sidewalk, totaling about fifty miles.

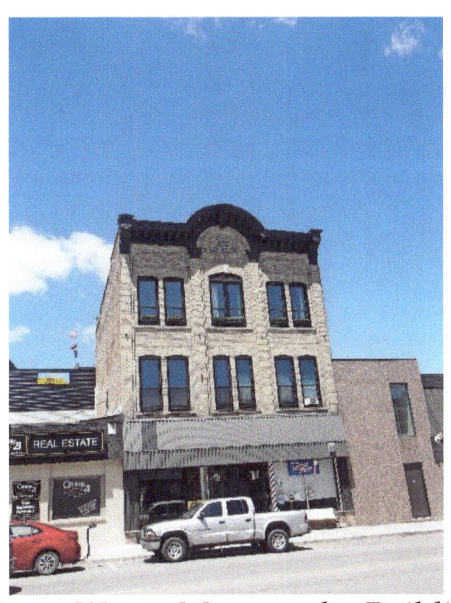

14 King Street West – Morsworthy Building – 1876

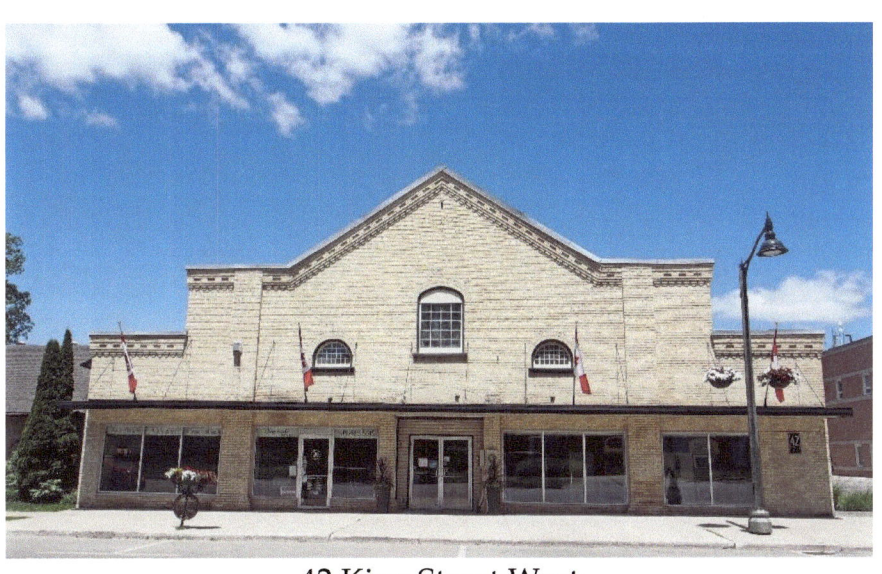

42 King Street West

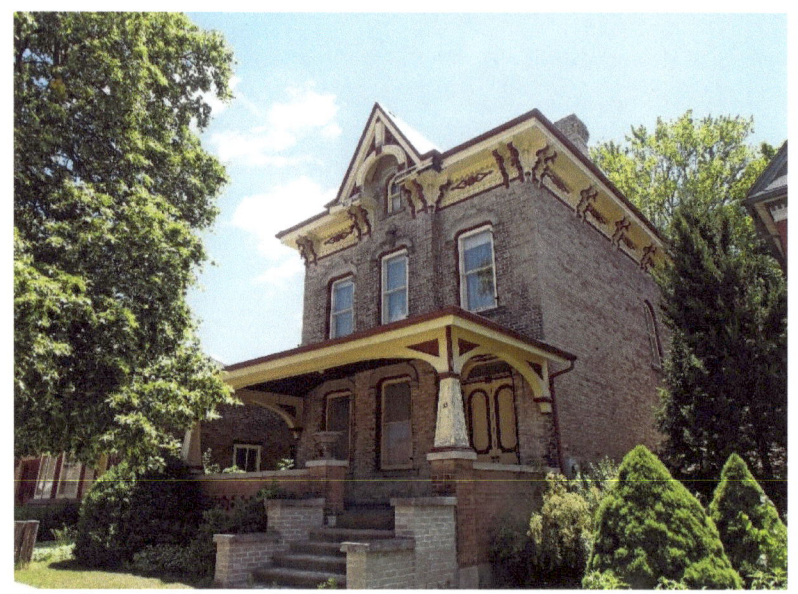

55 King Street West – Italianate - decorative gable and cornice with brackets

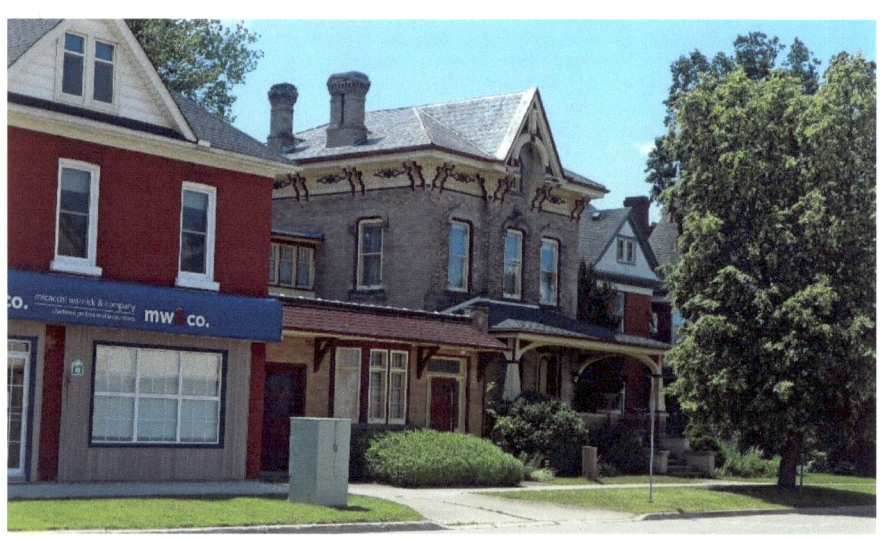

45 King Street West

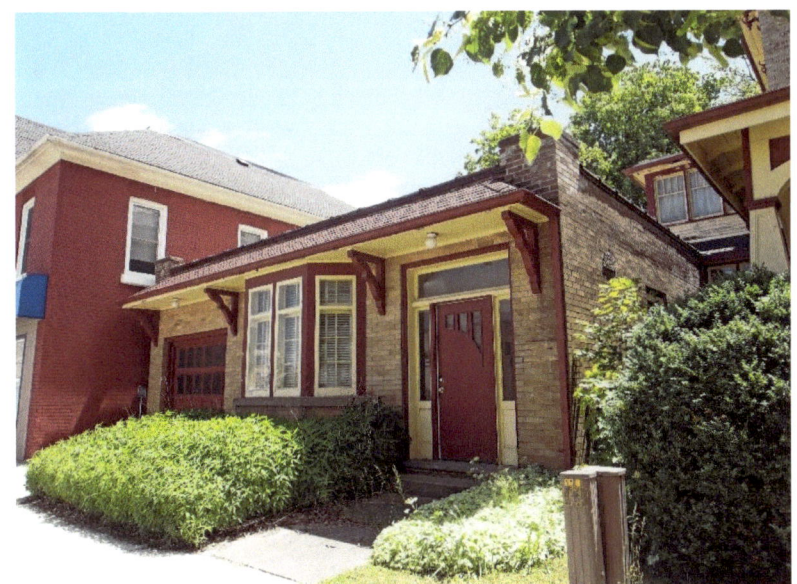

King Street West

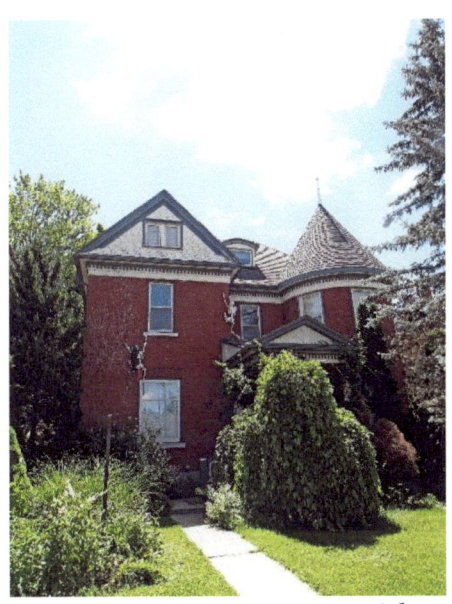

57 King Street West – two-storey tower with cone-shaped roof

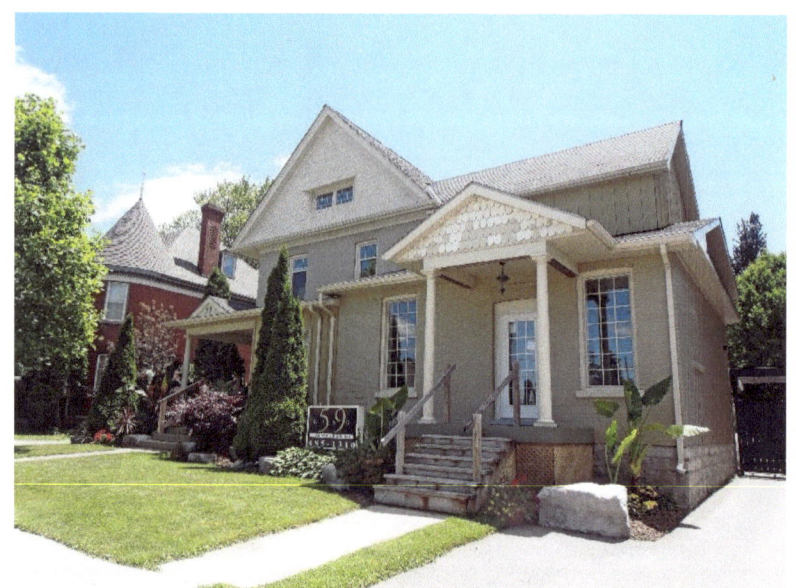

59 King Street West

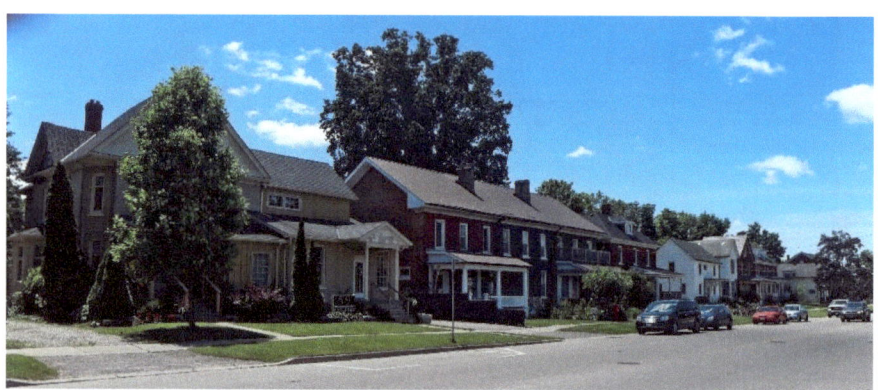

59-81 King Street West

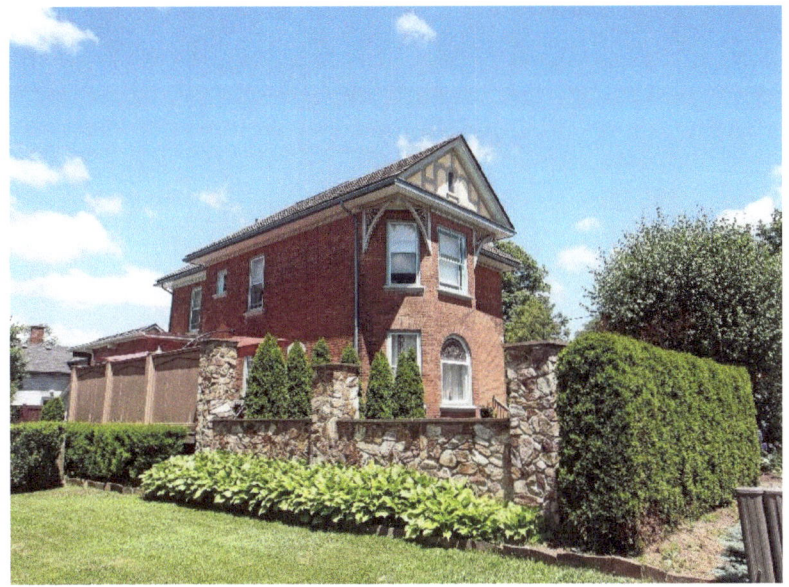

King Street West

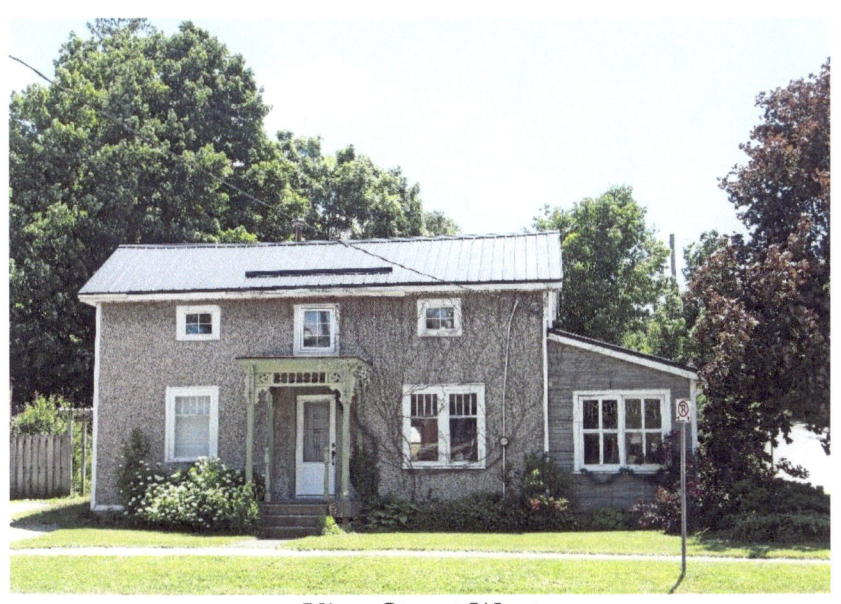

King Street West

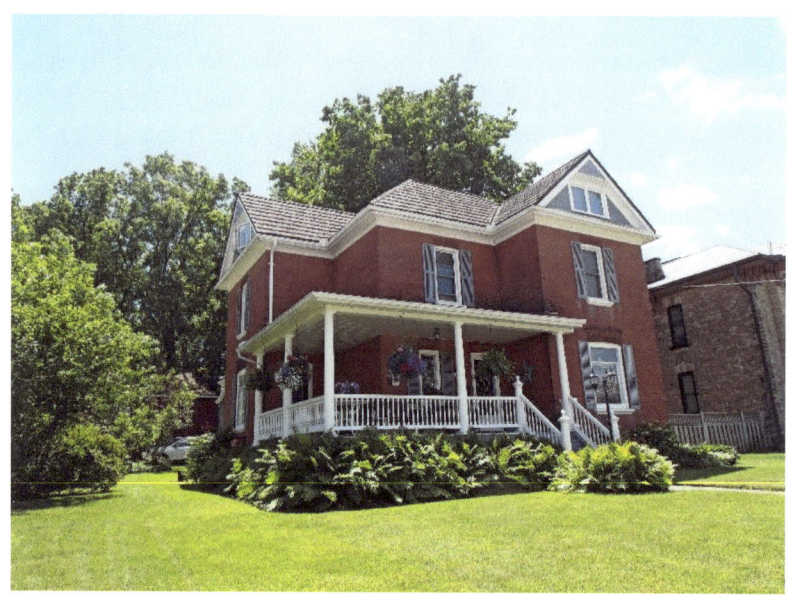

121 King Street West

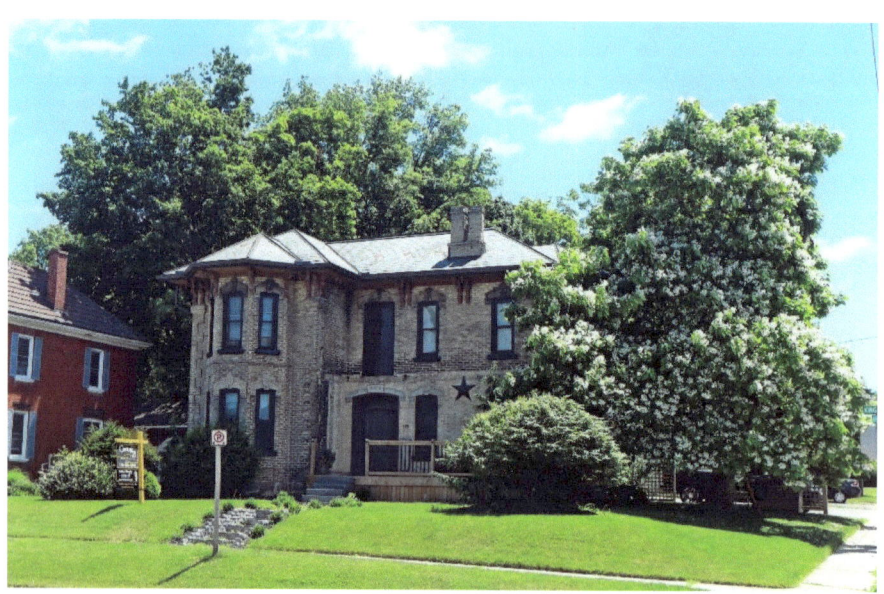

129 King Street West – paired cornice brackets, two-storey bay

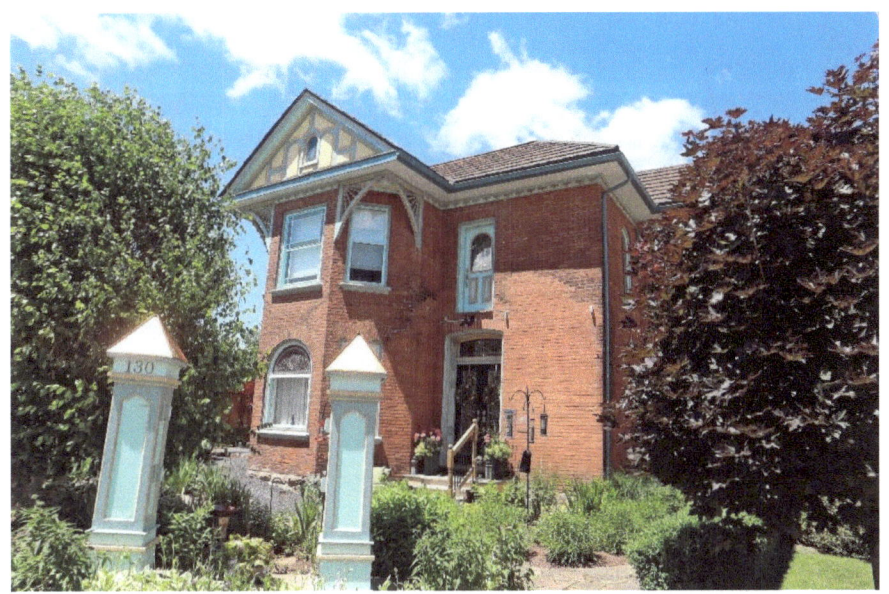
130 King Street West – 2½-storey bay with fretwork

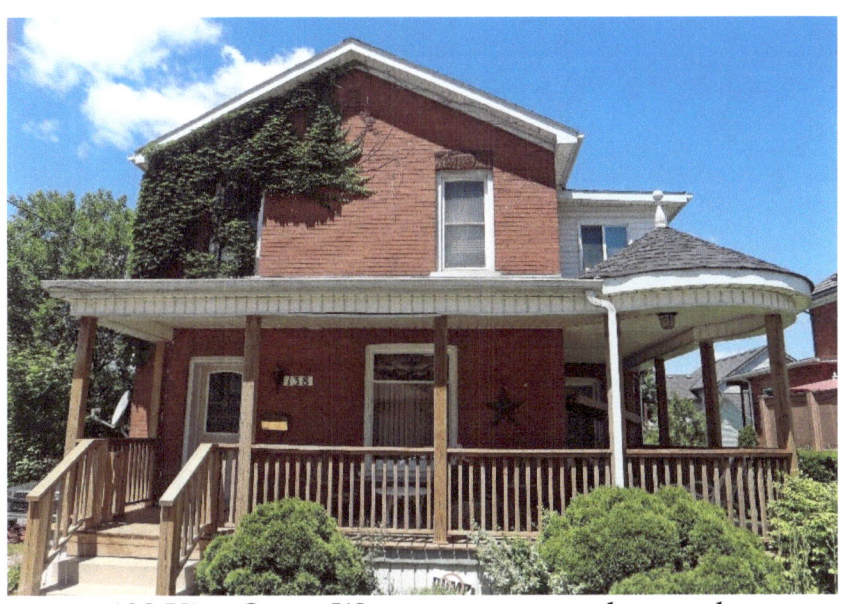
138 King Street West – wraparound veranda

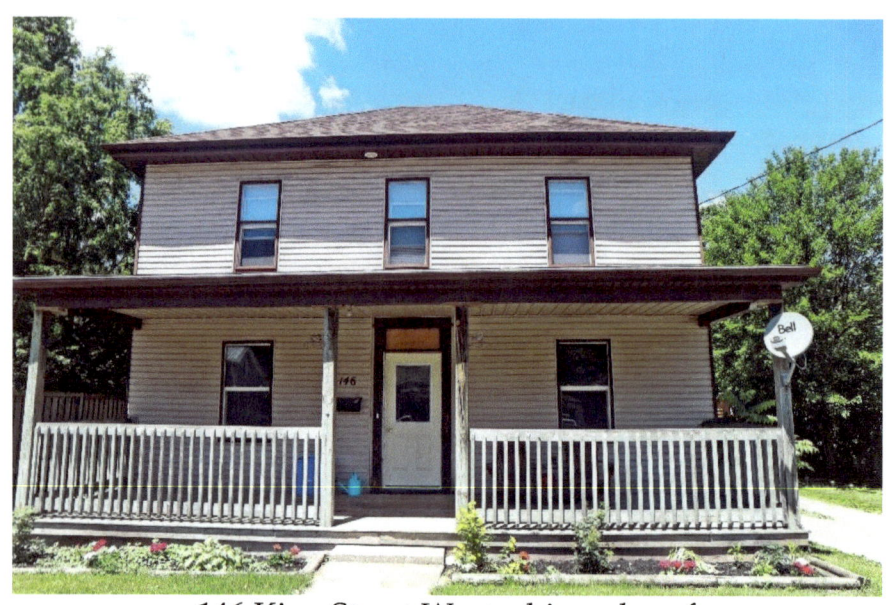
146 King Street West – hipped roof

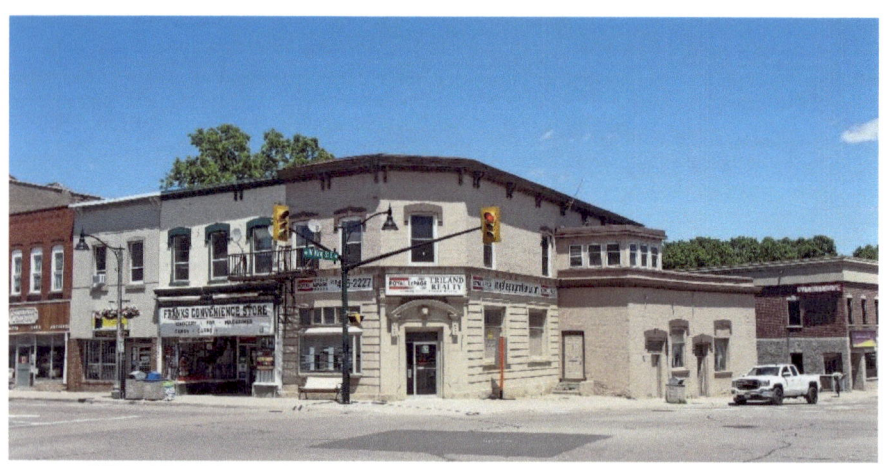
155-159 King Street West – paired cornice brackets

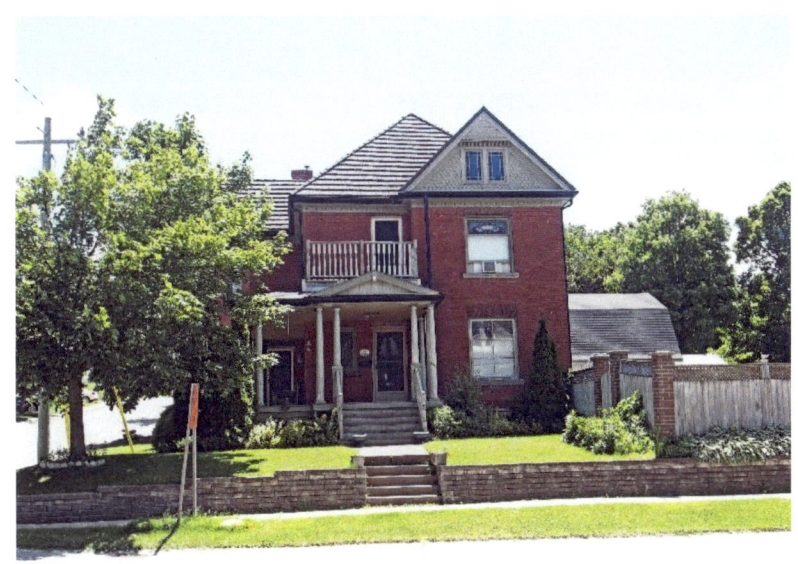

161 King Street West - Edwardian

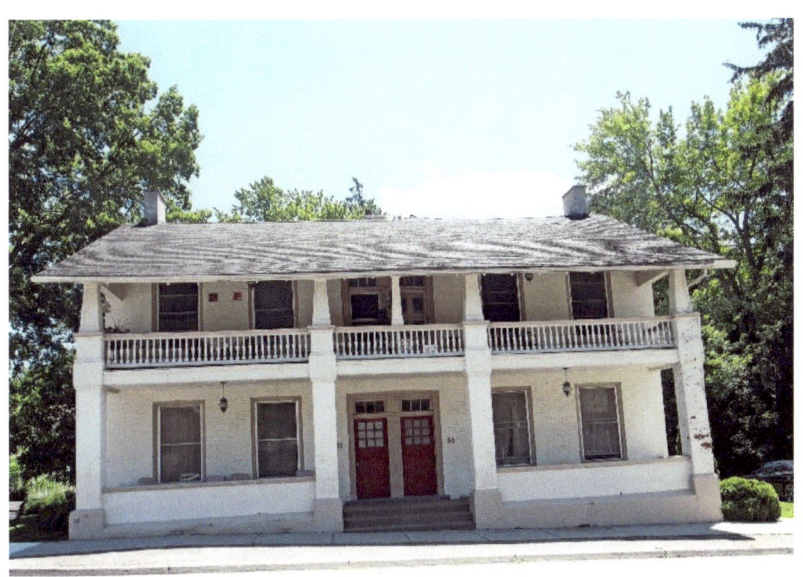

94-96 King Street East

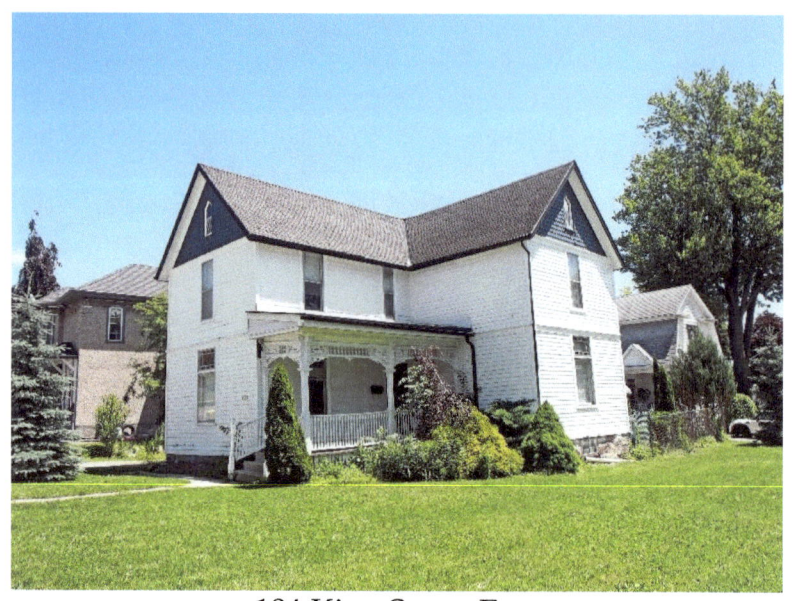
104 King Street East

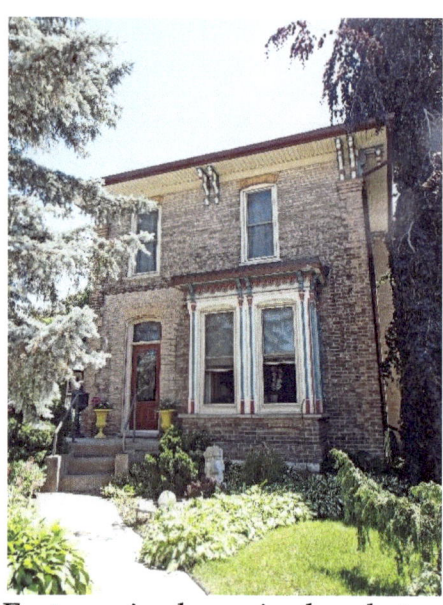
112 King Street East – paired cornice brackets, rectangular bay window with brackets

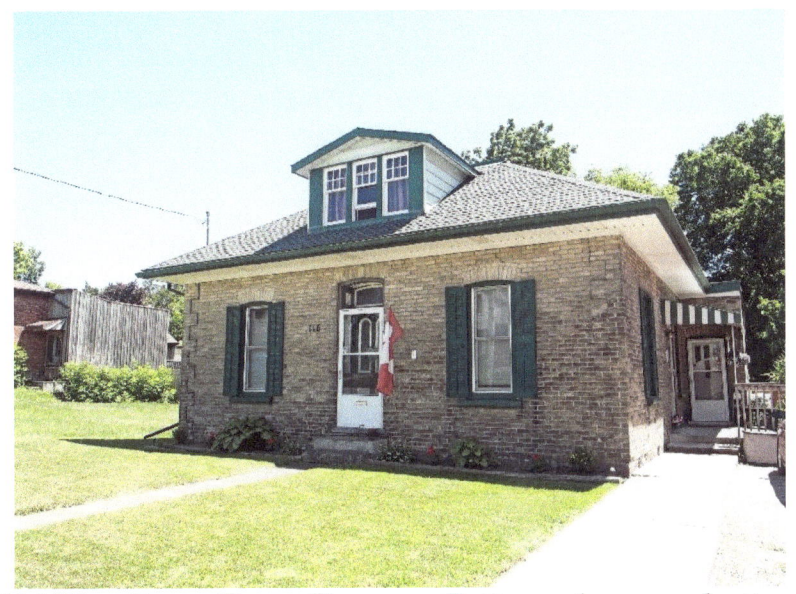

116 King Street East – Regency Cottage, dormer, shutters

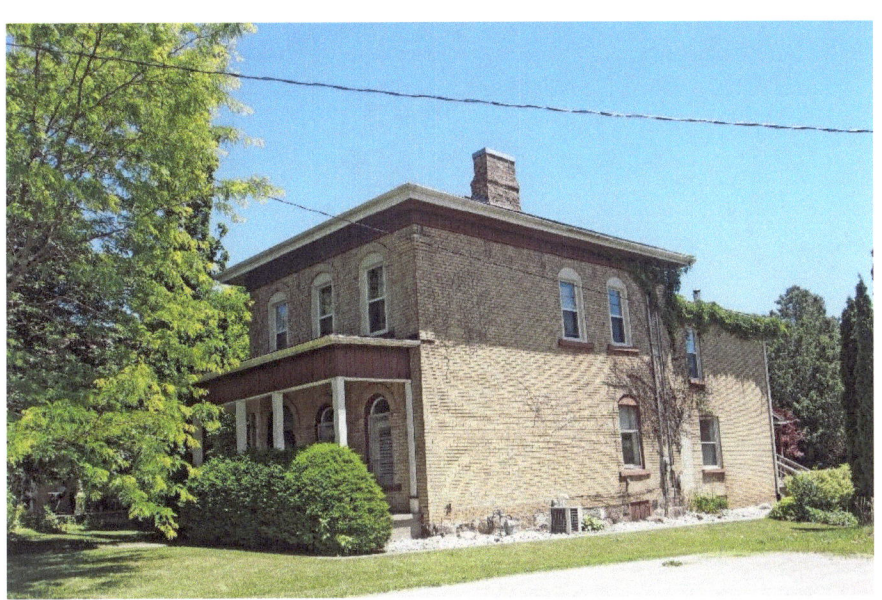

126 King Street East

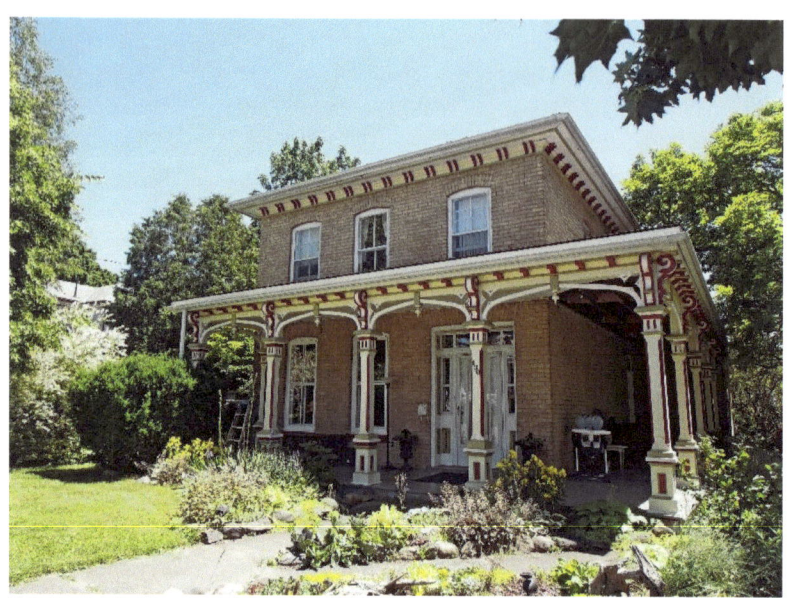

130 King Street East – decorative cornice on house and veranda

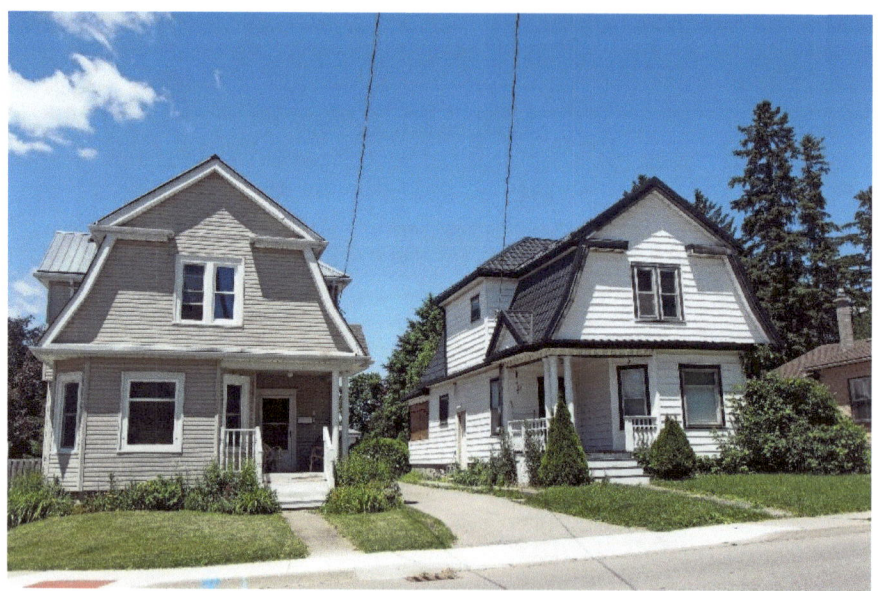

143 and 145 King Street East – Neo-Colonial style with gambrel roots

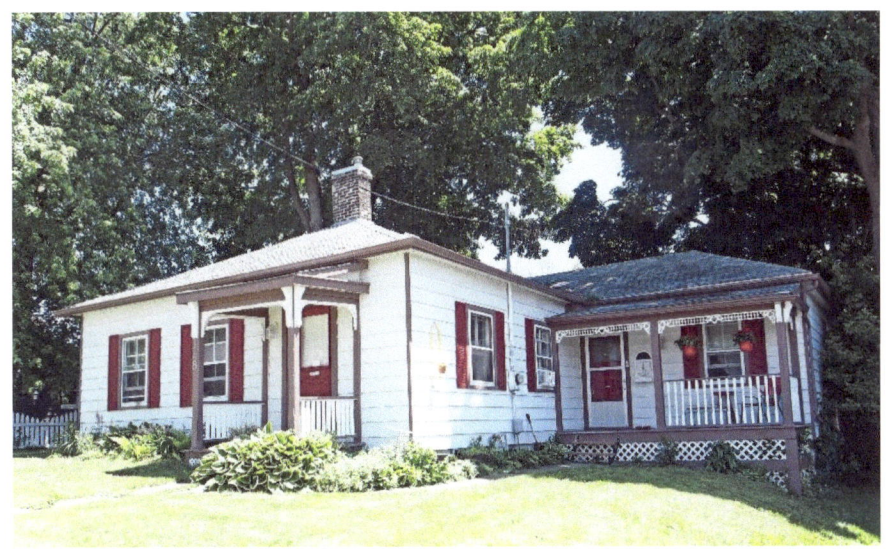

148 King Street East – Regency Cottage with side wing

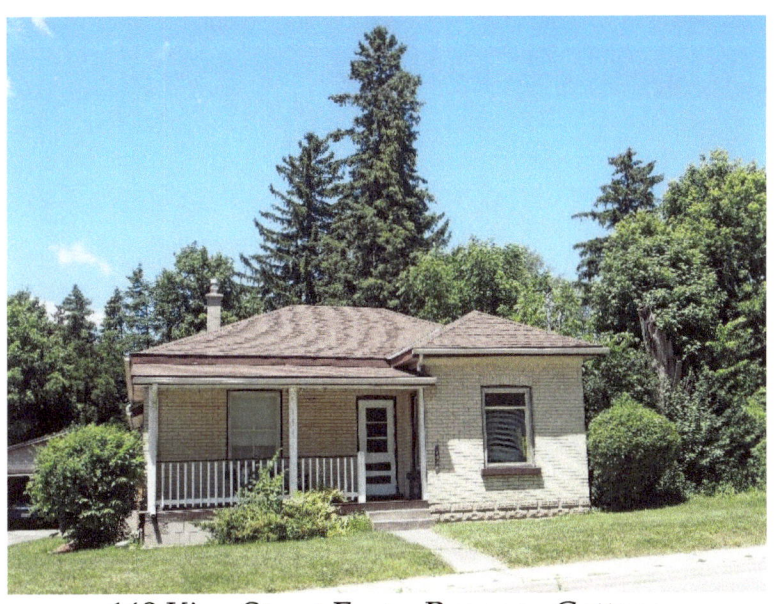

149 King Street East – Regency Cottage

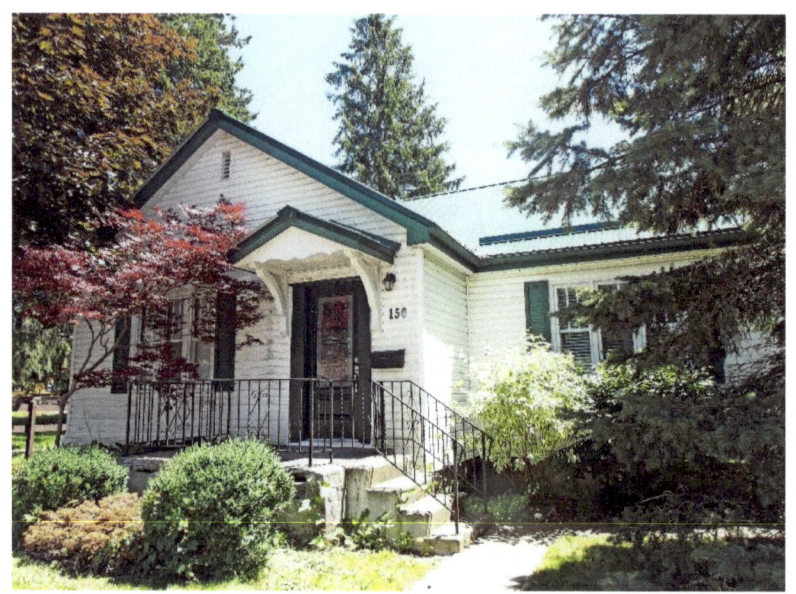

150 King Street East

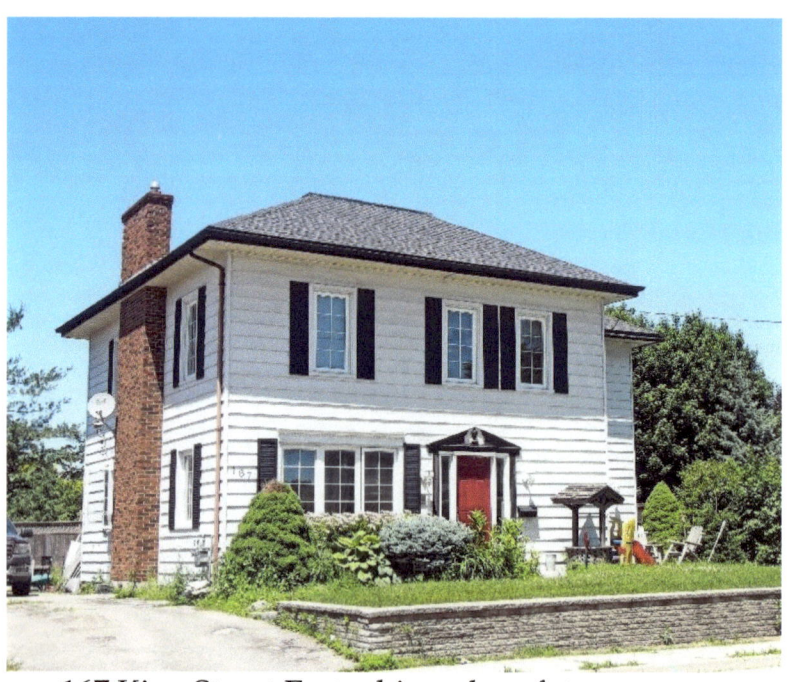

167 King Street East – hipped roof, two storeys

In 1608, French explorer Samuel de Champlain introduced the first dairy cattle to Canada. As more settlers arrived, the number of dairy cattle increased. French and English settlers used recipes they brought with them to make their cheeses. French made soft cheeses, and the English introduced cheddar cheese. Cheddar cheese is named after Cheddar, England. Much of this cheese was exported to England as the British would eat half a pound of cheese each at their noon meal.

In the 1830s, Lydia Ranney established Canada's first cheese making school on the family farm near Salford, Ontario. She trained many young men and women in the art of cheese and butter making. The students worked on the dairy farm in exchange for their schooling. In 1861, Hiram Ranney was the largest cheese producer for all of Oxford County and produced 30,000 pounds of cheese.

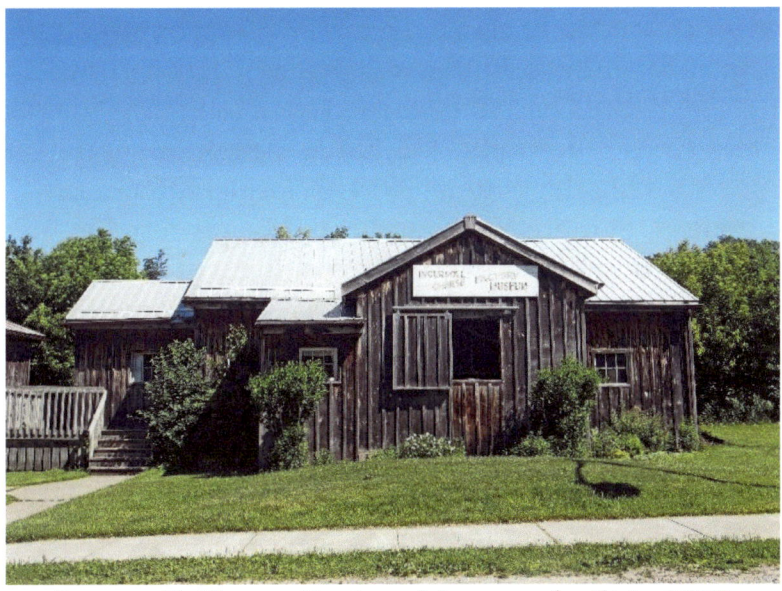

Ingersoll Cheese Factory Museum built in 1977

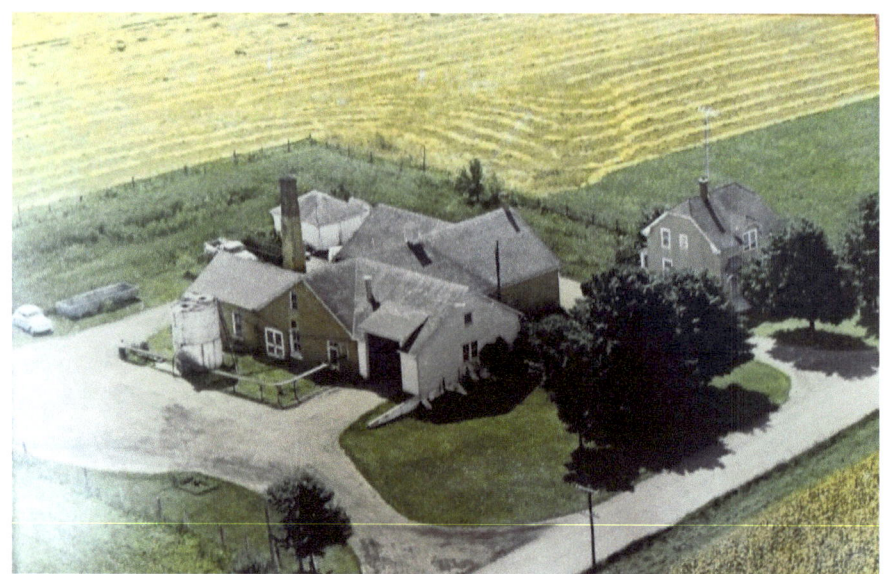

Canada's first cheese factory was built by Harvey Farrington in Norwich, Ontario in 1864. Farmers were now able to deliver their milk to the factory and have it made into cheese for them. Many cheese factories also produced butter.

In pioneer days, butter was made by hand in small churns. The paddle had to be turned for a long time to make both butter and buttermilk. A drain at the bottom of the churn was for removing the buttermilk. This large butter churn could make a lot more butter and could be powered by steam; people could buy butter instead of making it at home.

Milk cans were hoisted to the weigh-in vat with the aid of milk pail slings and a crane. The milk was poured into the vat and weighed. Sample portions were taken to be used in the Babcock Tester to determine the butterfat content of the milk. The Babcock Tester was made in 1882 as a result of farmers adding water to their milk which lowered the butterfat content and produced a runny cheese. In the Babcock Tester, heated milk samples were spun for five minutes which allowed the butterfat to float to the surface where it could be measured.

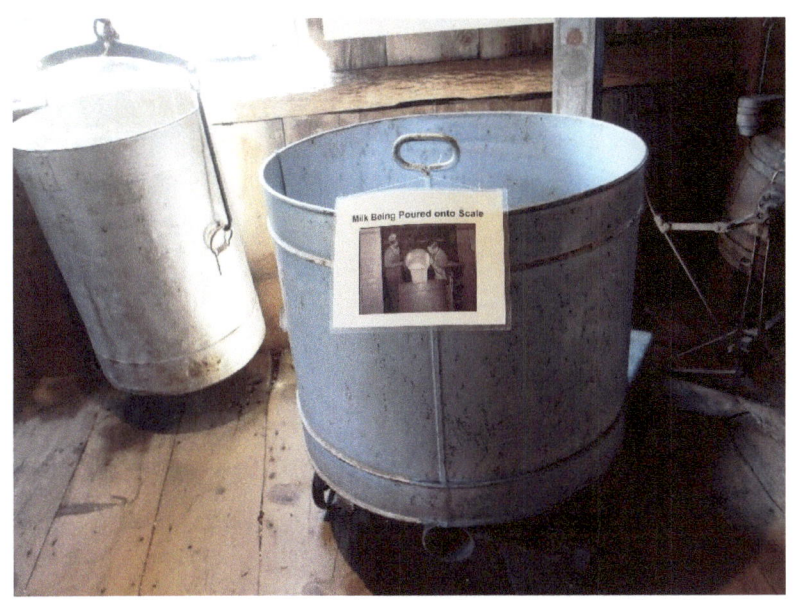

Milk was poured into scale to be weighed.

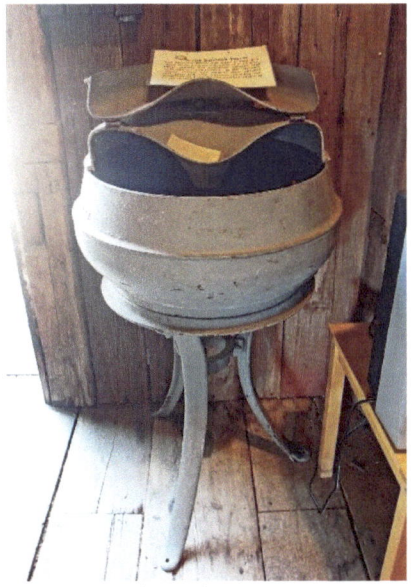

Babcock Tester

The boiler produced steam to power much of the equipment in the factory.

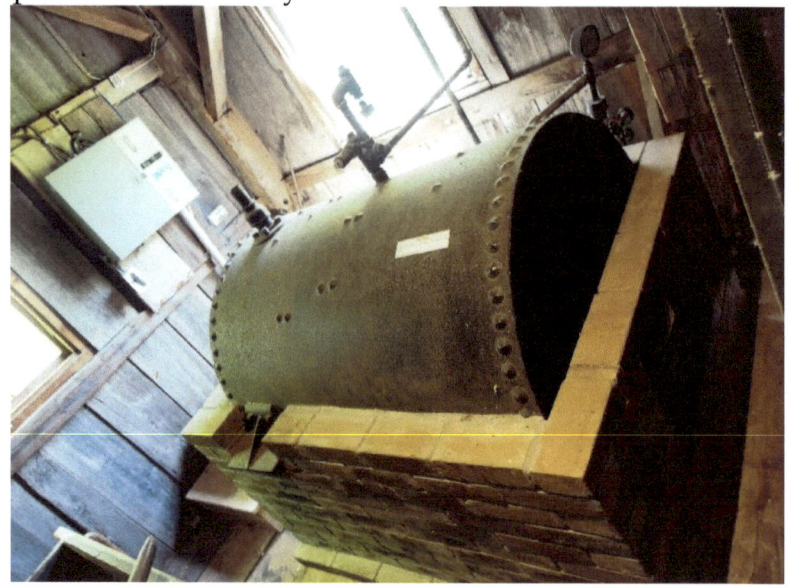

The milk carts could be pulled by hand for short distances or by dogs or horses. The pail in the center is suspended on the axle so that it will swivel. This allows the pail to remain level to ensure that the milk does not spill when being transported.

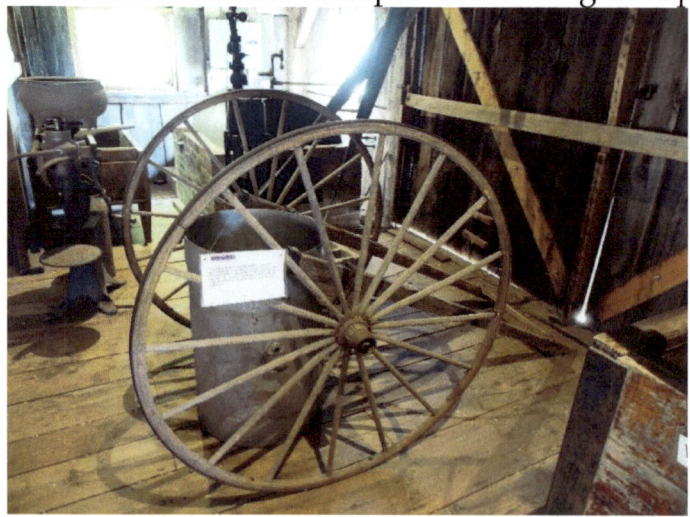

The curing room was usually in the basement of the cheese factory as the temperature had to be maintained at 15 degrees Celsius. The lower the temperature, the better the cheese. The rounds of cheese were placed on curing shelves or in curing boxes to cure. The cheese would be turned and greased daily to prevent moisture loss. Cheese aged for two to three months is considered "mild" or "medium" and cheese cured for twelve months or longer is sold as "old" or "well-aged" and cheese cured for 18 months is known as "extra old".

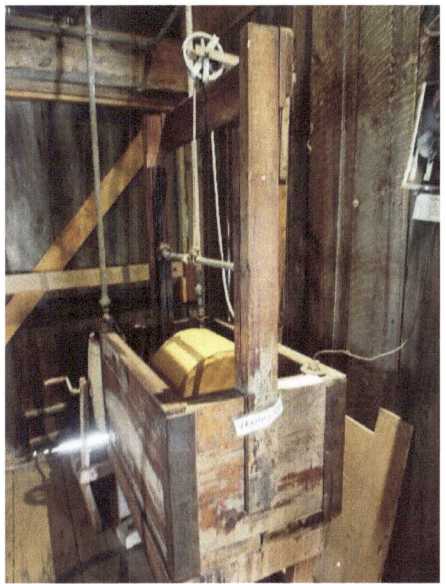

Before they were wrapped, wheels of cheese were lowered into a vat of hot wax. The coating suspended the curing process and helped to preserve the cheese.

Cheese Stamping Table – The word "Canada" is visible on the 58 pieces of type which signified that the cheese was intended for export.

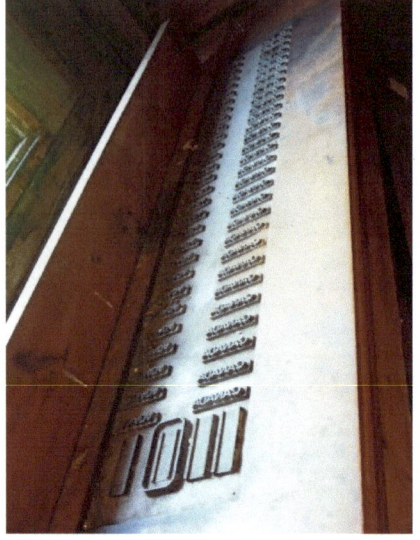

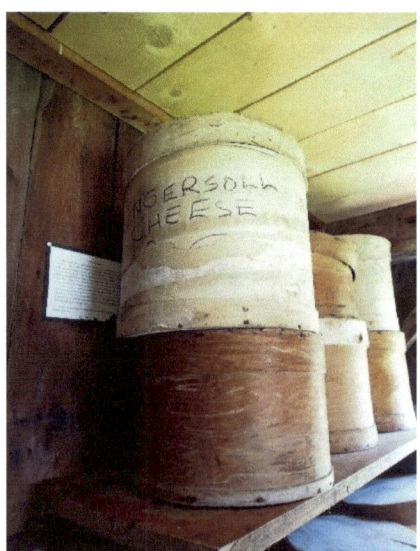

Early cheese blocks were sixty pounds; later they were ninety pounds.

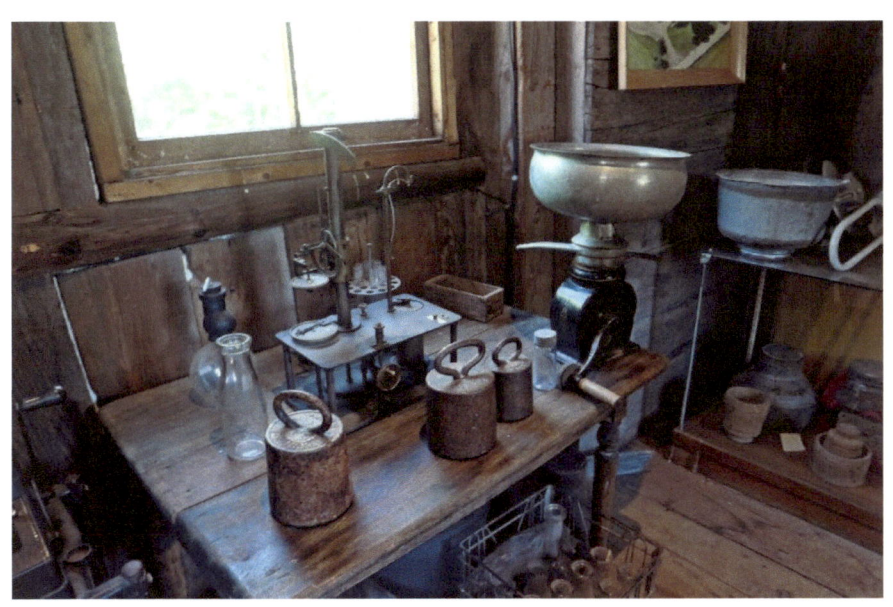

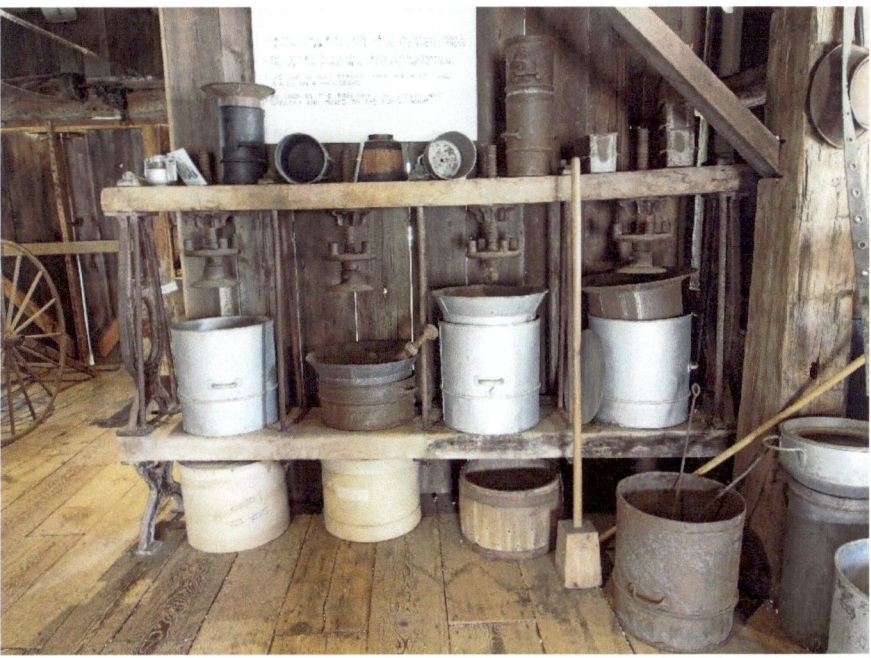

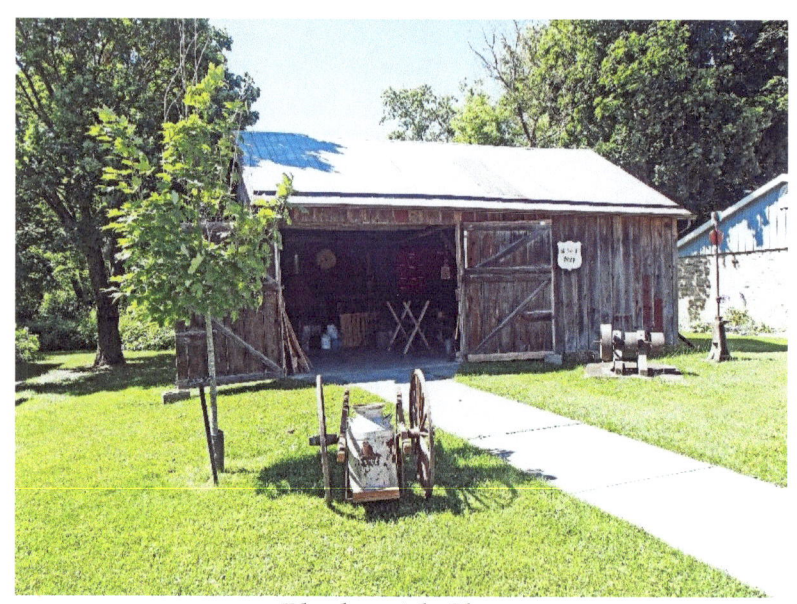

Blacksmith Shop

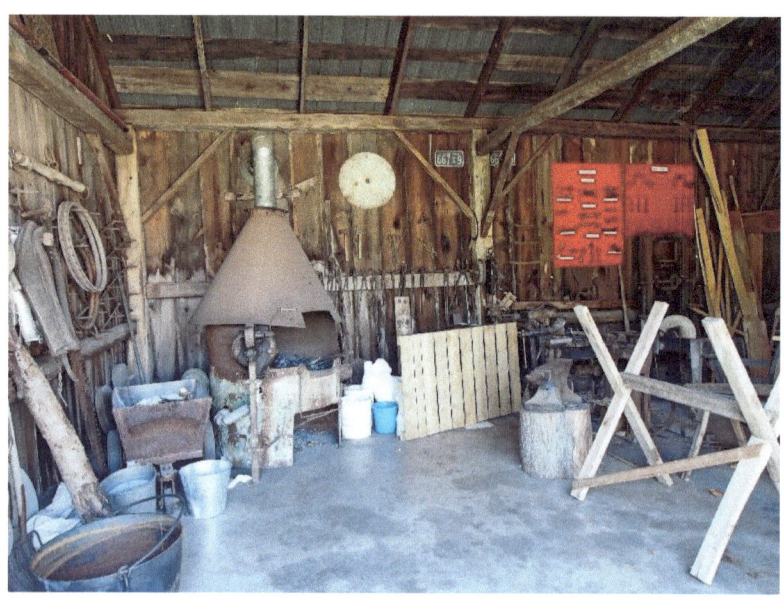

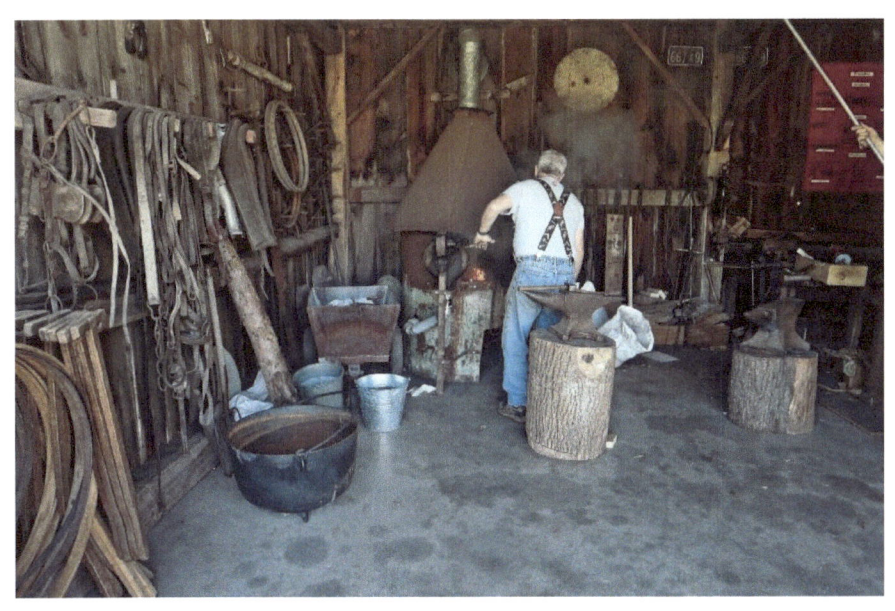

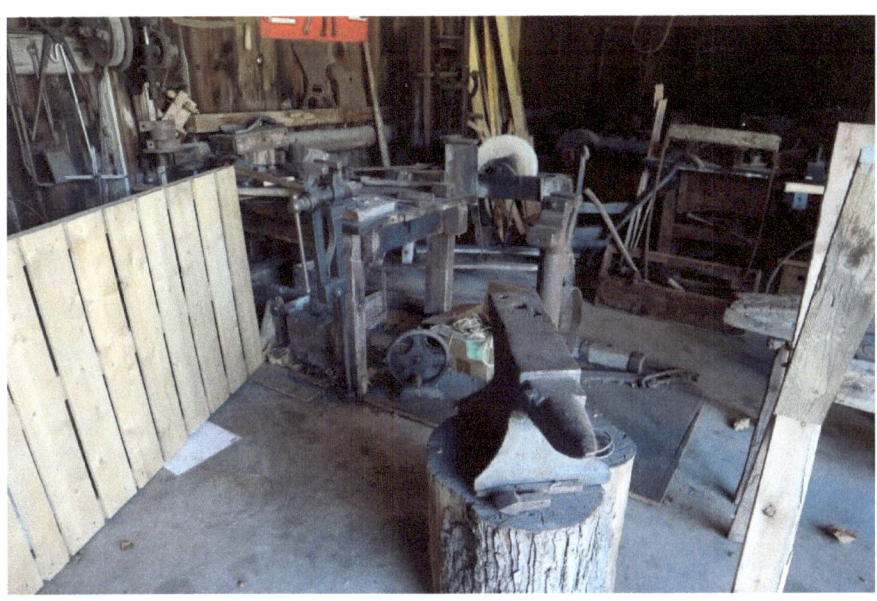

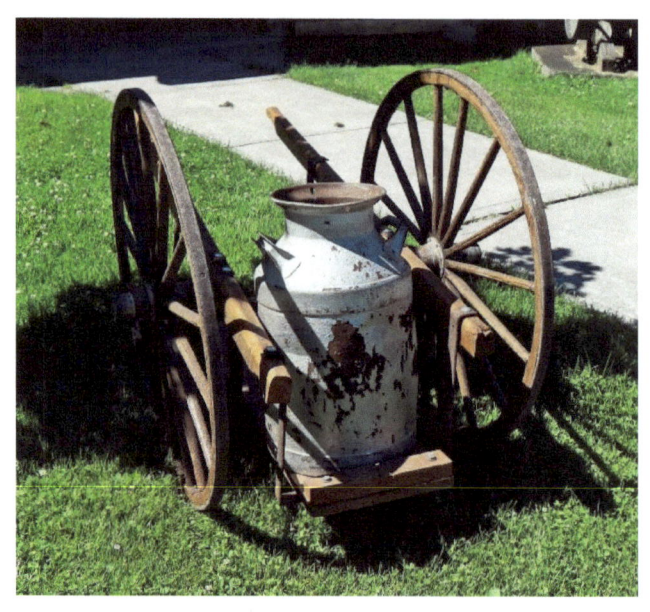

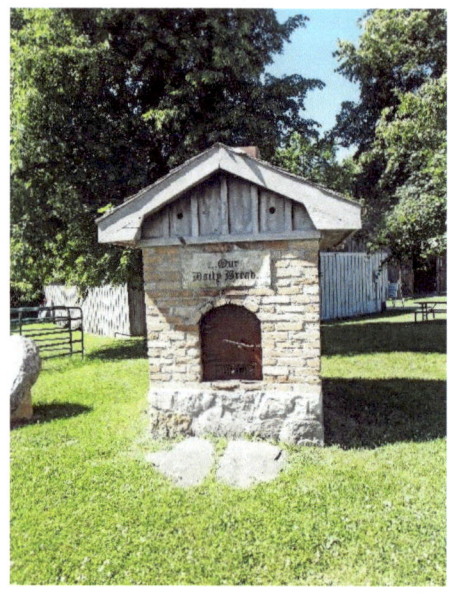

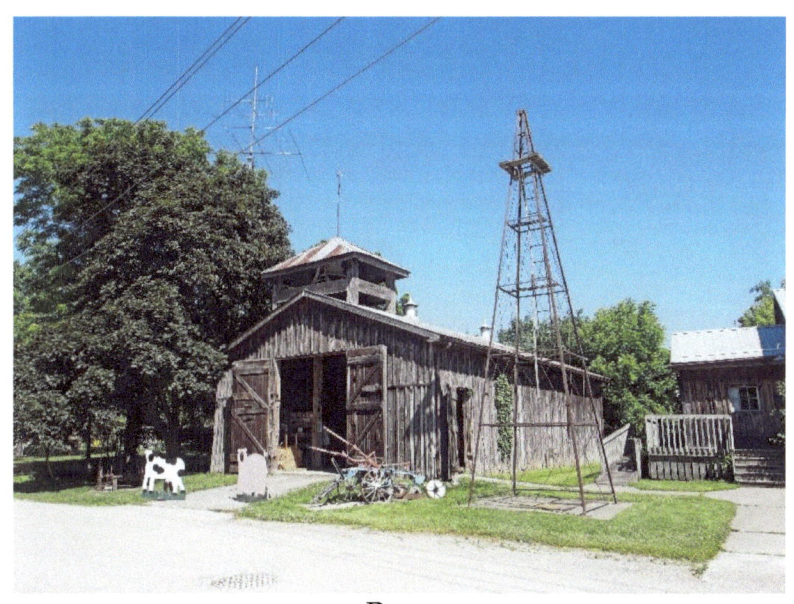

Barn

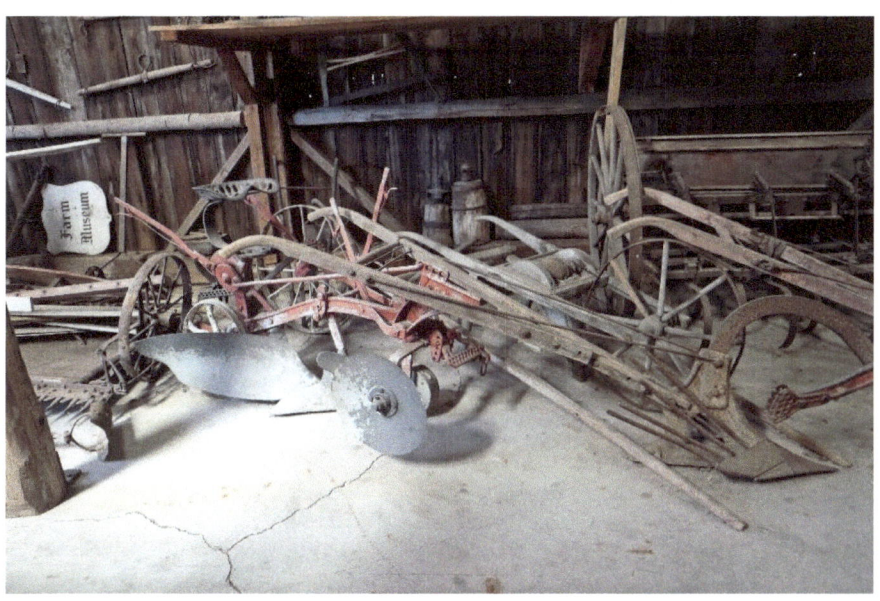

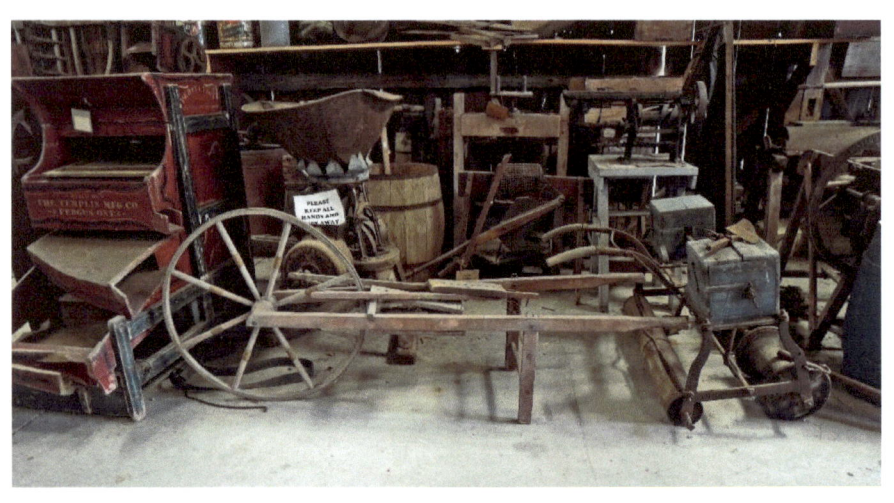

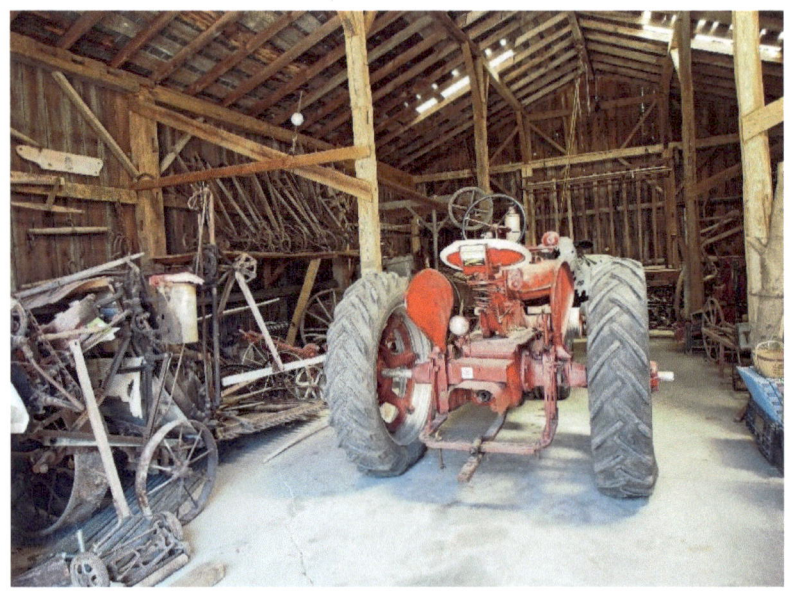

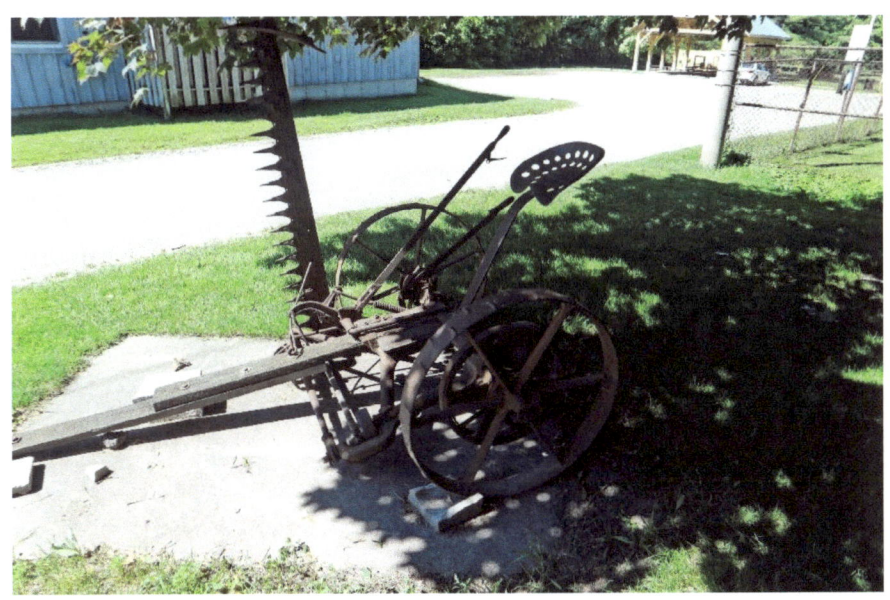

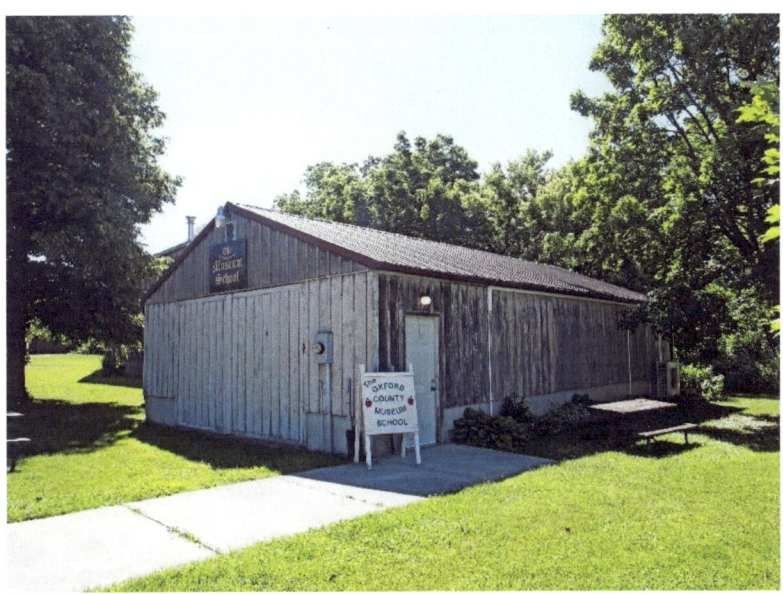

The Oxford County Museum School

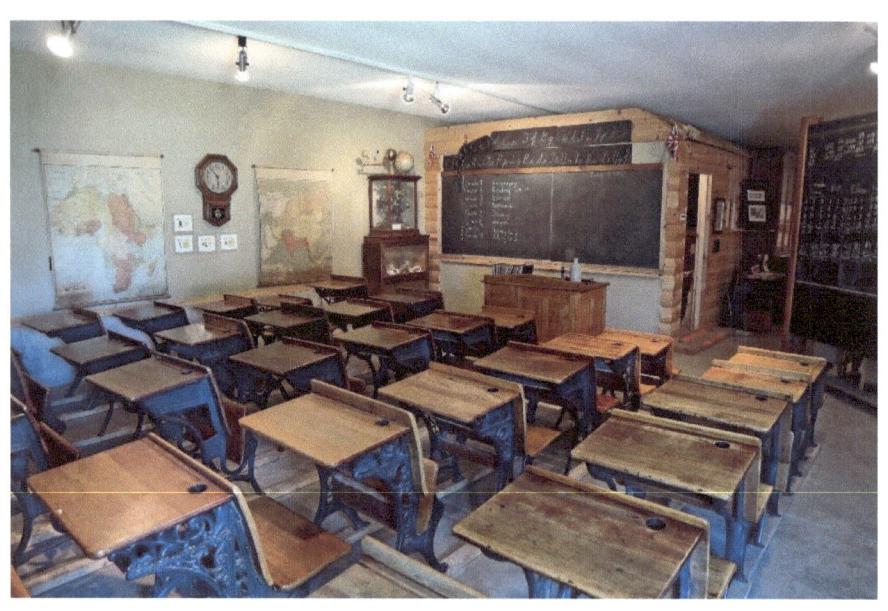

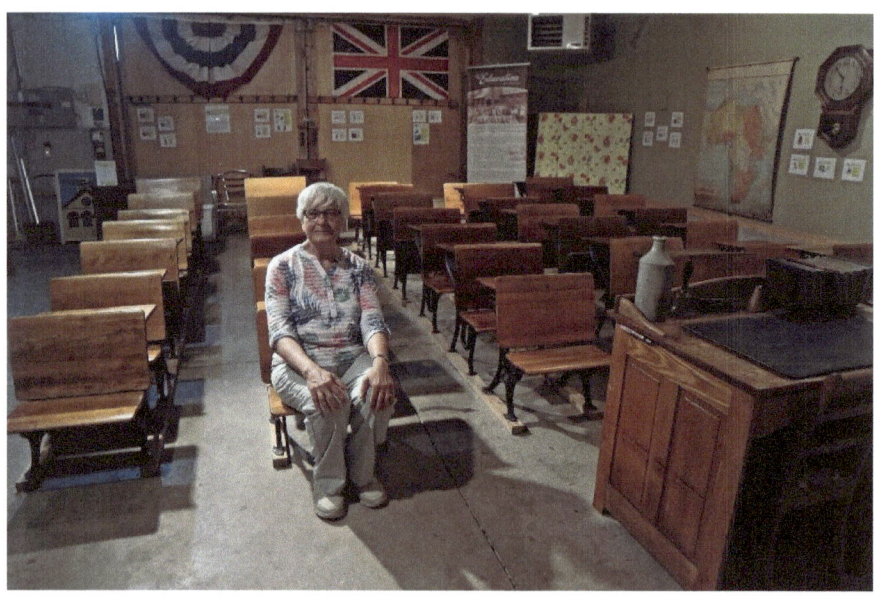

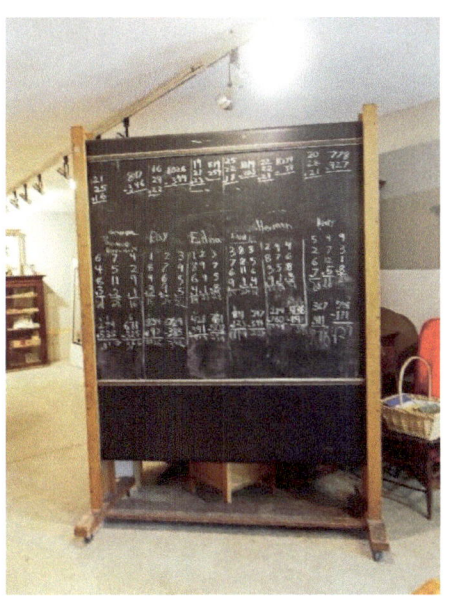

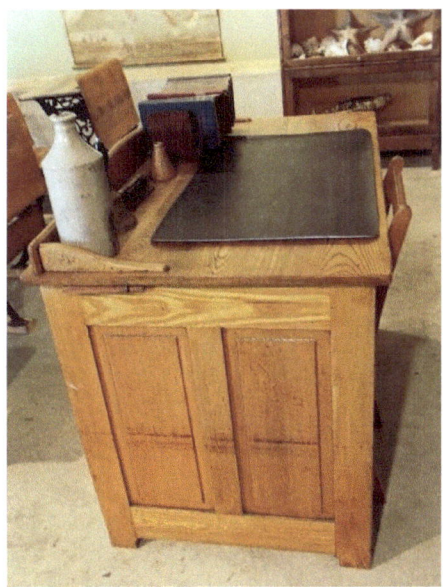

Teacher's desk

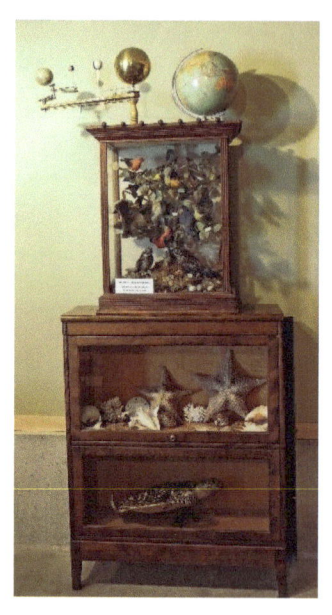

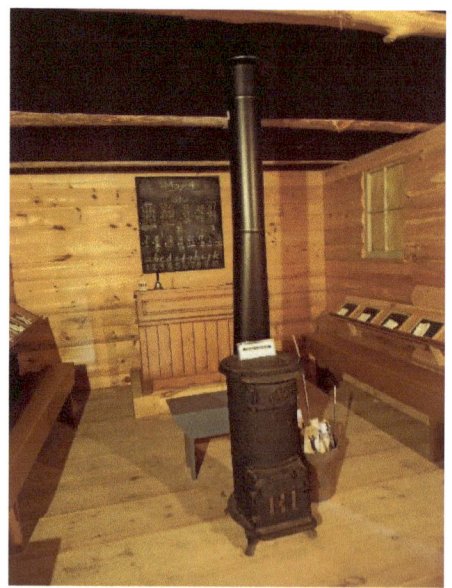

Stove for heating

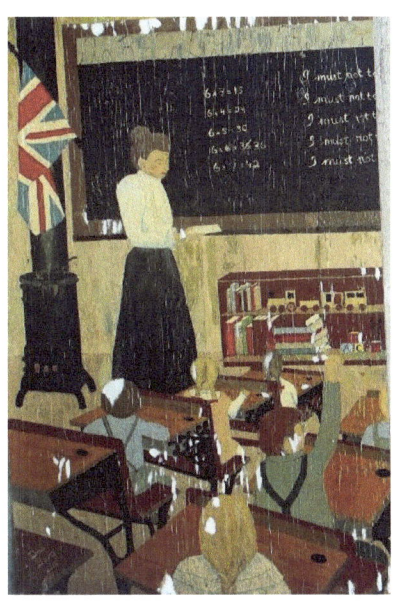

Murals

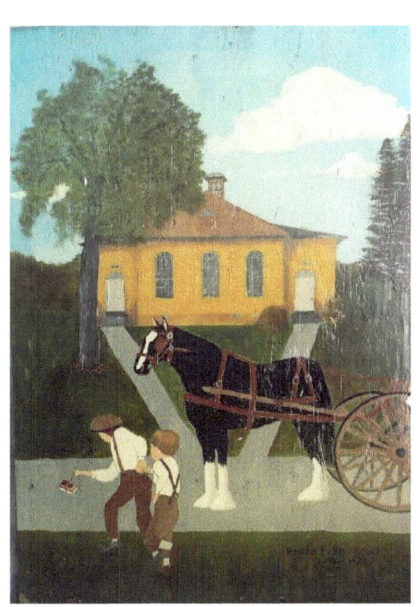

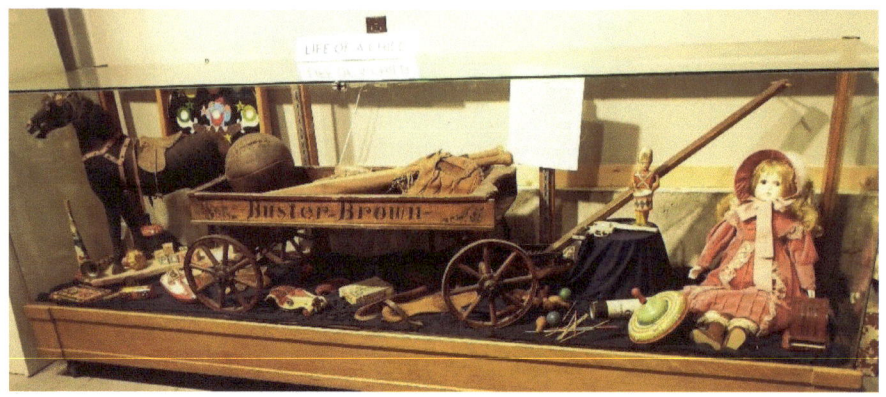

Toys – In the early years of settlement, children were not indulged much as there were always plenty of chores to do. By the eighteenth century, children enjoyed a bit more free time and played with an assortment of toys from dolls to stilts. Many were homemade but the majority were imported from the established toy shops of Europe. Toys were expensive and considered rare and precious treasures.

The Industrial Revolution brought in the age of mass-produced and disposable toys. New materials such as plastics and cheap metals were introduced into the toy maker's warehouse. Children were able to enjoy a greater variety of playthings than ever before. By the 1850s, every city and many small towns had a toy store.

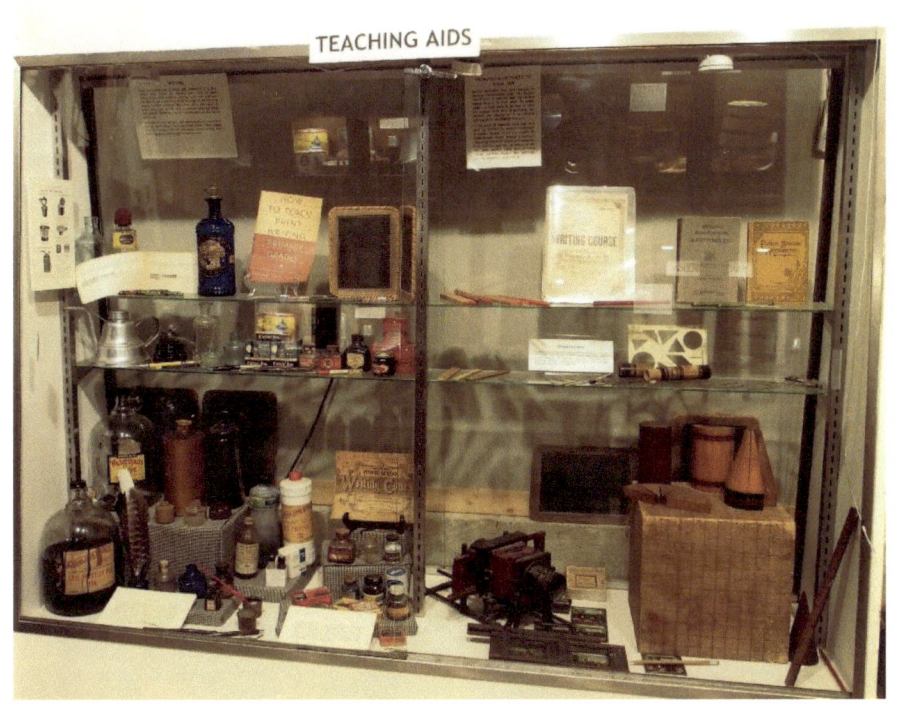

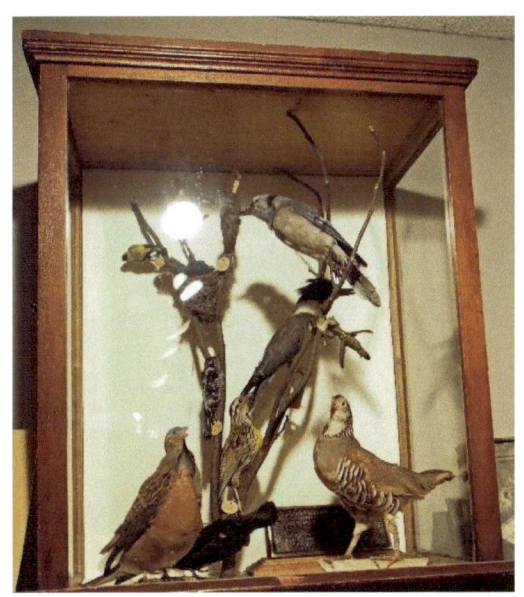

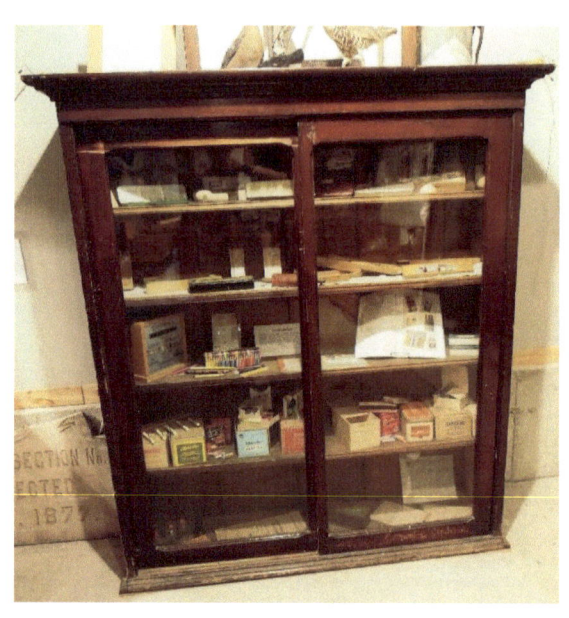

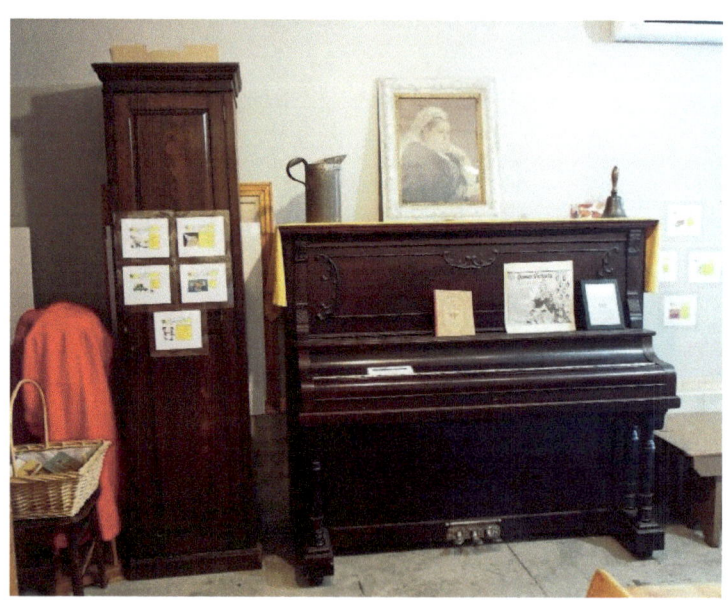

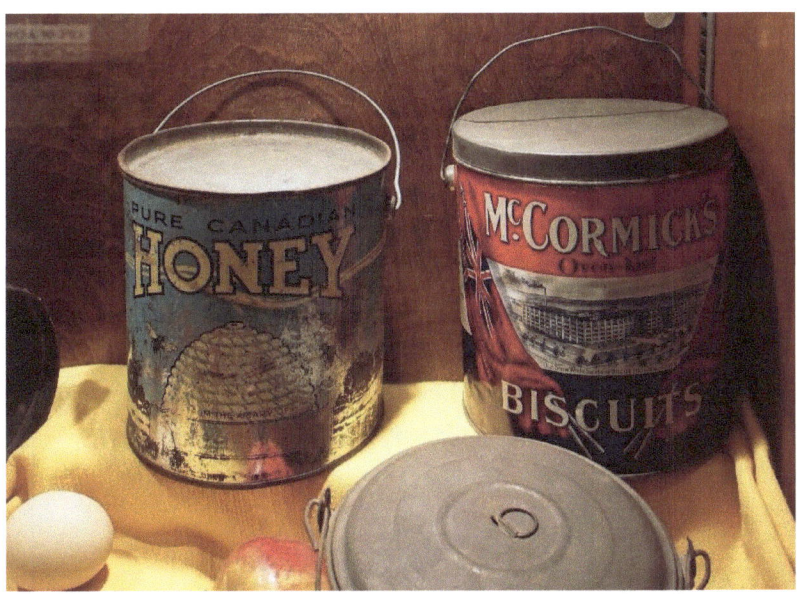

The first lunch containers were re-used food containers the contents of which were such perishables as tobacco, biscuits, or lard. Any container was suitable as long as it could close tightly to preserve the contents until lunchtime. Manufacturers realized their product packaging was being used for this and they began designing containers with pictures painted on the tin surfaces. Children drank water from the school water jug with a drinking cup they brought with them.

Early school lunches would have included bread and butter sandwiches, hard boiled eggs, seasonal fruit and vegetables, preserves. Later there was meat, cheese, milk, cake and cookies in a student's lunch pail.

The first pioneer schools appeared in Upper Canada in 1811 – often a deserted building or log structure. There were few trained teachers. The subjects taught were agriculture and business. Reading, spelling, writing, and arithmetic were all that was necessary. School fees were often paid by providing wood for the schoolhouse, or lodging for the teacher.

As time passed, the schoolhouses increased in size and number. Maps, globes, blackboards and scientific equipment became standard in the 1850s. By the 1870s, girls were admitted on equal terms with boys as education became compulsory for all children aged 7-12 but only for four months of the year. Schools were provincially funded and controlled. They were required to have a fenced play area, water, and outhouses for both boys and girls. These improvements were part of the standards outlined in the School Acts of 1846, 1850 and 1871 by Rev. Egerton Ryerson, Chief Superintendent of Education. He was also responsible for developing the first Ontario Readers for Canadian students to replace British, Irish, and American textbooks. He established schools for training teachers.

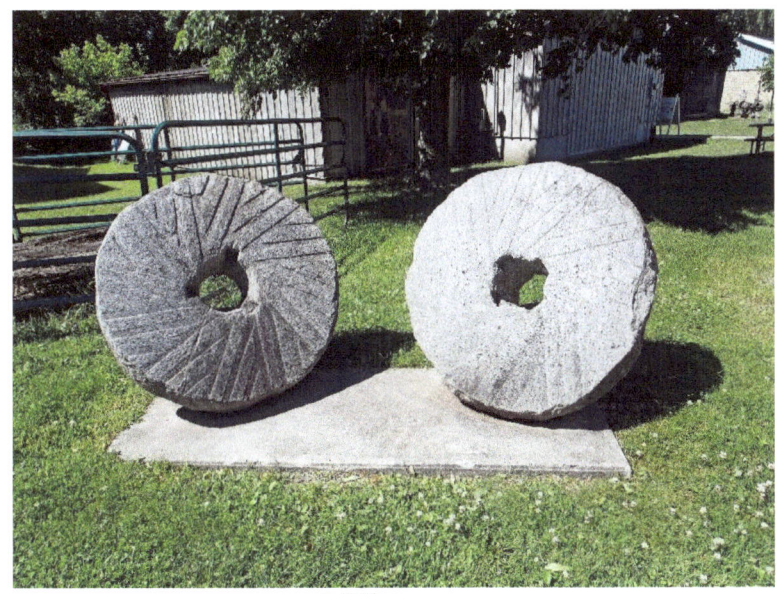

Millstones

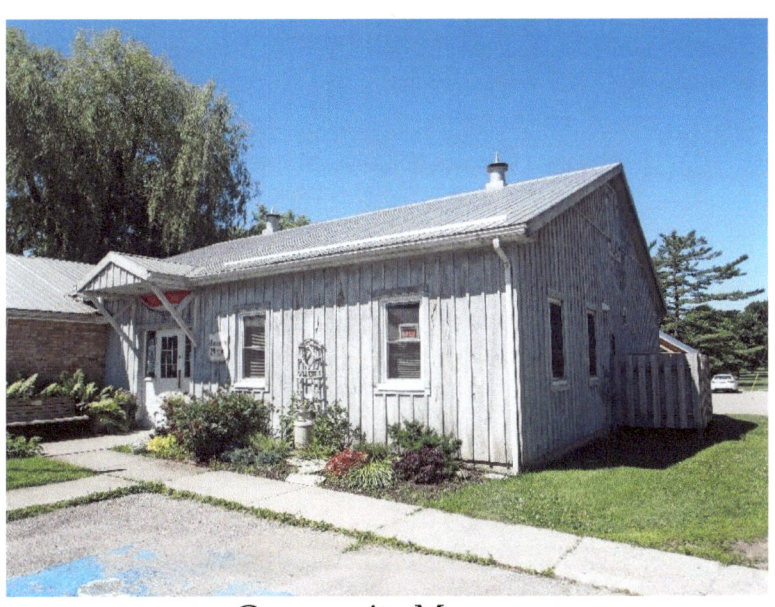

Community Museum

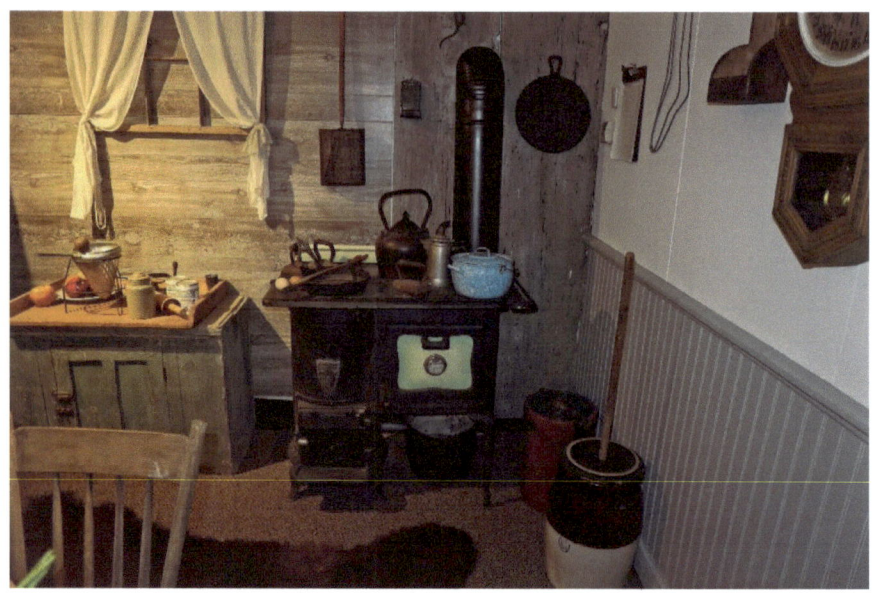

     Born in 1749, Thomas Ingersoll was one of eight children who represented the fifth generation of Ingersolls in America. He became a successful merchant in Great Barrington, Berkshire County (near the New York border).

     Thomas Ingersoll was a Republican supporter during the American Revolution. He rose to the rank of Major. He requested an honorable discharge from the militia on January 20, 1795 in order to move to Canada to settle. They moved to Queenston on the Niagara River and he opened and operated a tavern which provided the family with an income and shelter while he was away initiating the Oxford settlement.

     During his time in the new settlement, Thomas acted as a local Justice of the Peace. He was instrumental in the development of thirty miles of road which connected Burford to the Thames River. On July 25, 1802, Thomas was appointed Captain of the Oxford County Militia.

When Thomas left the settlement in 1805 and relocated to Etobicoke Township, he leased a tavern called the "Government Inn" and operated a ferry on the Credit River until his passing in 1815. It was at this Inn that Thomas provided food and accommodations for representatives of the Mississauga First Nation and officials from York (Toronto) for the signing of the "First Purchase" Treaty.

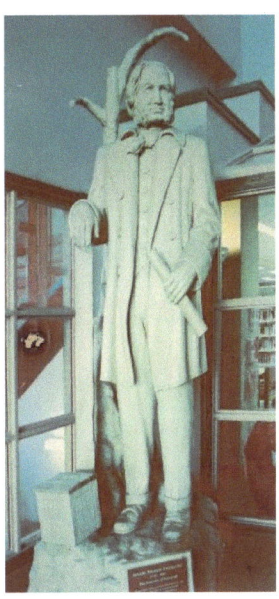

Charles Ingersoll was the eldest son of Thomas Ingersoll and Sarah (Whiting) Backus and was born in Great Barrington, Massachusetts on September 27, 1791. During the War of 1812, he volunteered for the militia and served as Quartermaster of the Niagara Light Dragoons. He later partnered with Captain William Hamilton Merritt and formed the Provincial Light Dragoons for which he served as Lieutenant. The company fought in actions at River Raison of Maumee, Fort George, Stoney Creek, Black Rock, and Lundy's Lane. For his service, Charles received a grant of land following the war.

In 1821, Charles returned with his family to the Oxford homestead. He served as Postmaster and Justice of the Peace.

Both Charles and his brother James were influential in the restoration and development of the Ingersoll settlement.

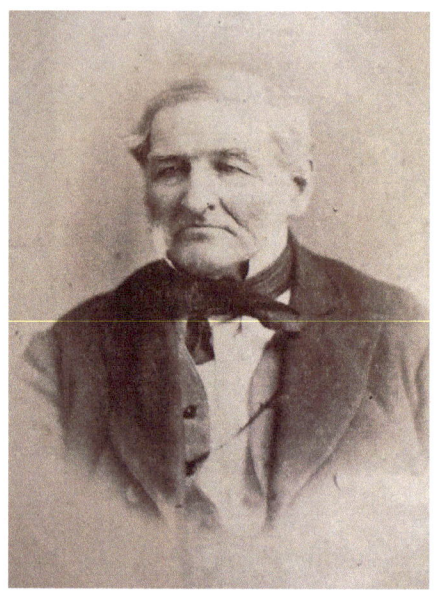

Thomas Ingersoll had been introduced to Chief Joseph Brant of the Six Nation Reserve during a visit to New York. Upon learning about Ingersoll's disappointment with the *"harsh treatment of the Loyalists"* following the American Revolution, Chief Brant made an offer to Ingersoll to show him the ideal place to start a settlement if he ever wished to come to Canada. When Ingersoll arrived in Canada, he took Chief Brant up on his offer, and the Chief arranged for six of his best men to escort Ingersoll to the River la Tranche (now the Thames River). Brant said that this land was once a summer camping ground for the Mohawk Indians and it was some of the finest land in this part of Canada.

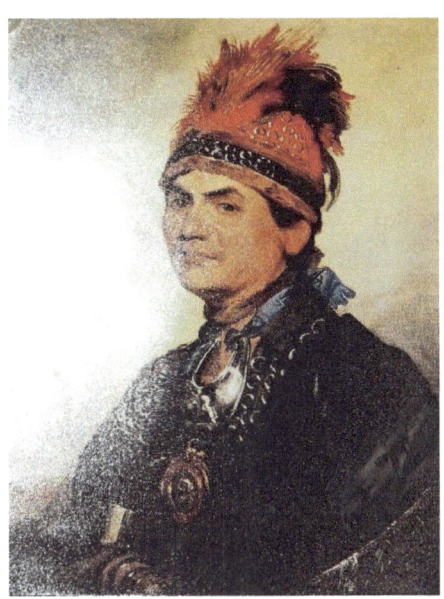

Chief Joseph Brant

Colonel Charles Ingersoll founded the village of Lakeside, East Nissouri Township. Charles was granted large tracts of land in Oxford for his service during the War of 1812. His son, Squire James Ingersoll, played an active role in the formation of the community. His uncle, William Carroll, already owned land near the present village, and James saw the potential of the site and purchased three hundred acres on the northern edge of the lake in 1835. In 1842 a public building was erected which served as a school for many years. James undertook the building of the village's first brickyard in 1859, a grist mill and saw mill in 1860 and donated land for the Anglican Church and cemetery. The village continued to grow and included a hotel, a blacksmith shop, tailor shop, ashery, shoe shop, and carpenter shop.

Shortly after the establishment of Upper Canada in 1871, newly appointed Lieutenant-Governor John Graves Simcoe issued a proclamation which offered land grants to Loyalists and other subjects who would develop large tracts of unsettled land in the province. Thomas Ingersoll applied for a land grant and was awarded 66,000 acres in what was to become East, West, and North Oxford Townships. A condition of the land grant contract was for him to settle forty settlers in the new settlement. Each family that settled in the district was sold a parcel of up to two hundred acres of land at a cost of six pence per acre.

Thomas used his own money to pay for the surveying of the townships, for clearing the land and for building roads. These were necessary to encourage citizens to come to the newly formed settlement of Oxford-on-the-Thames (later called Oxford Village). Thomas moved his family to Etobicoke Township in 1805.

After the War of 1812, Thomas' four sons, James, Charles, Thomas Jr. and Samuel returned to Oxford County to carry on their father's dream of a settlement here. It was renamed "Ingersoll".

James, Thomas Jr. and Samuel Ingersoll were influential in the founding of St. Marys. They built a saw and grist mill on the east side of the Thames River. Thomas' son John opened the first store. Thomas donated land for the building of the first Presbyterian and Anglican churches in the settlement.

On February 28, 1775, Thomas Ingersoll married seventeen-year-old Elizabeth Dewey and they had four children, with the eldest being Laura (Secord) born in 1775 who became a famous Canadian heroine of the War of 1812.

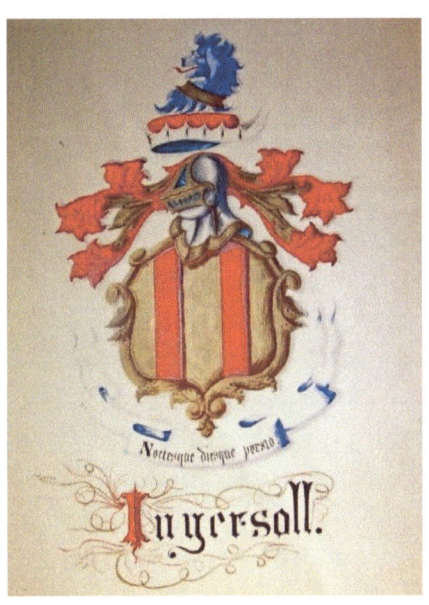

Ingersoll Family Crest – The Ingersoll family is of Saxon origin and the Arms of the family originated in Norfolk County, England. The center of the Arms consists of a gold shield that is dissected with two red Pallets (stripes) and upon the "Cap of Dignity" is a red crest and a lion's head which is blue with a gold collar.

The Ingersoll family received the Arms for capturing two field fortifications from the enemy. The two red Pallets (stripes) represent these two fortifications and the red denotes "the great slaughter that took place." The gold field identifies that a great accomplishment was made, which brought much nobility and honor to the family.

The "Cap of Dignity" represents the amount of land once held by the Ingersoll family which equaled the amount of "two knight's fees in England." Before the conquest of the Normans in 1066 A.D., the family held the position of Lesser Barron and during the time of King Charles II, the position of Barron which qualified them to sit in the counsels of the Sovereign.

Laura Secord (nee Ingersoll) was born on September 13, 1775 and she moved with her family to Canada in 1795. In 1798, Laura married Captain James Secord and remained in Queenston after her family moved to Oxford County.

In the latter part of the War of 1812, her home was occupied by American soldiers. On June 21, 1813, Laura overheard plans for an attack on Canada. Early the next morning, Laura started on a dangerous thirty-two-kilometer journey by foot through the woods and fields from Queenston to Beaver Dams to warn British Officer James Fitzgibbon of the impending attack on his outpost. That evening she crossed Twelve Mile Creek and came upon a band of Chaughnawaga Indians. After explaining her plight, the Indian Chief took Laura to Fitzgibbon. Two days later on June 24, 1813, Fitzgibbon secured the surrender of the American invaders.

Fitzgibbon produced at least three certificates that verified Laura's role in the victory. Unfortunately, she didn't receive official public recognition for her heroic deed until her 85th year. It was during a visit to Canada by Prince Edward VII in 1860, that he presented Laura with one hundred pounds sterling for her bravery.

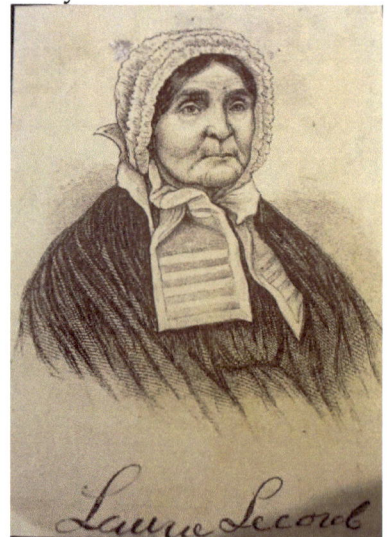

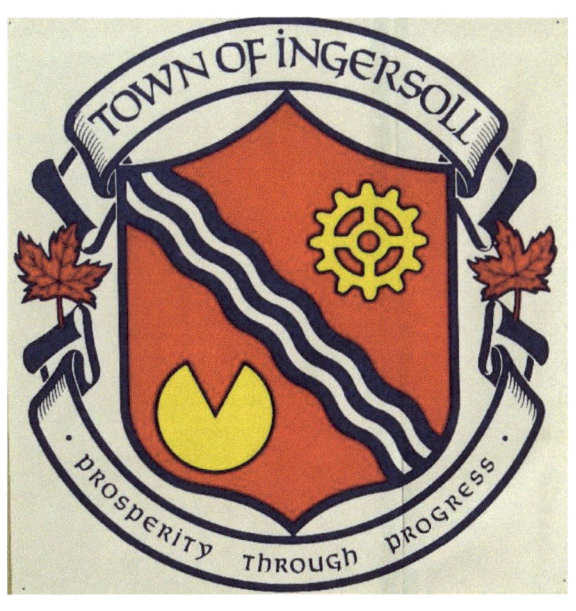

Prosperity Through Progress

The Town of Ingersoll logo reflects the community's unique history, heritage and industry. The red background of the crest is symbolic of the Town's association with the Empire Loyalists led by Thomas Ingersoll who came north after the American Revolution and settled in this area. The two maple leaves that flank the sides of the crest reflect the town's loyalty to Canada. The block of cheddar in the lower left of the crest symbolizes Ingersoll as Oxford County's cheese capital between the 1850s to the early 1900s. The cog symbolizes the town's industrial core. The center of the crest consists of blue and white waves which represent the peaceful flow of the Thames River which flows through the center of Ingersoll.

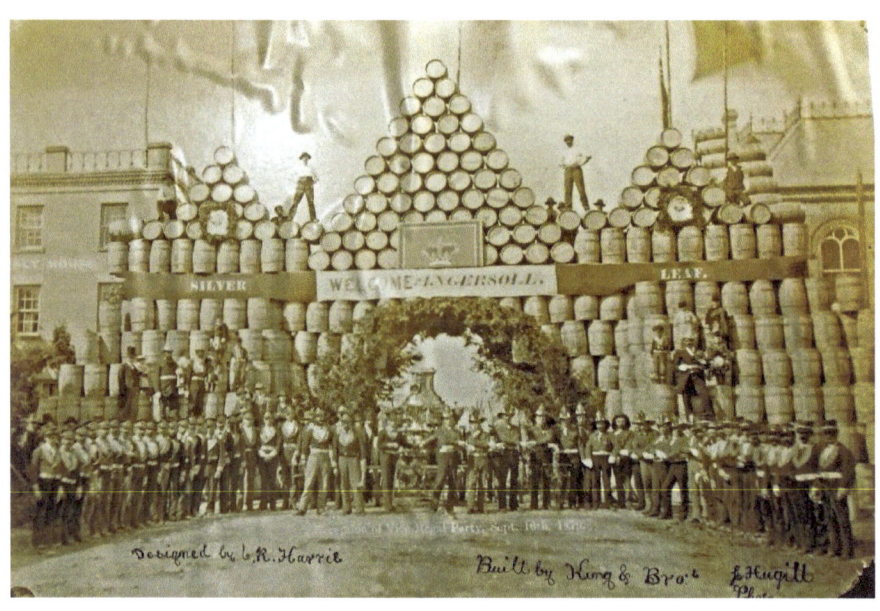

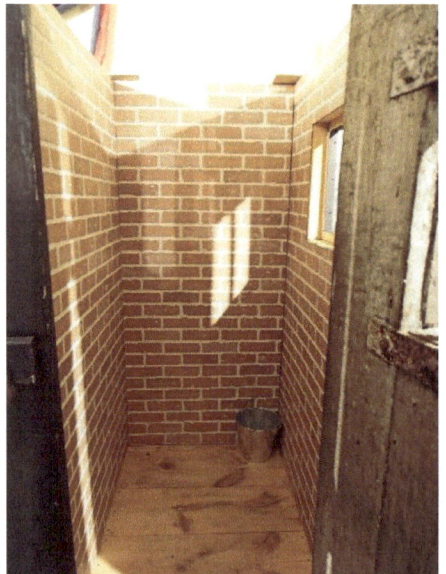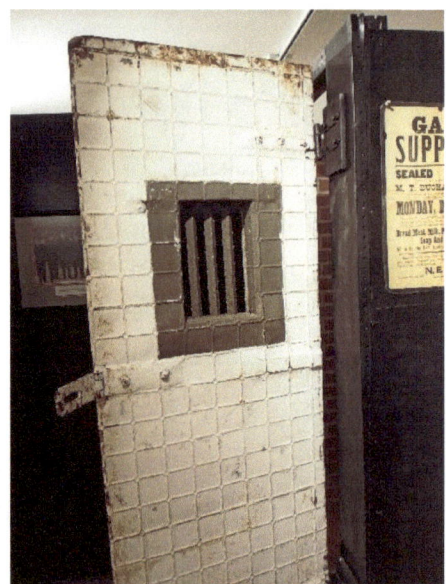

Jail cell

The first Great Western Railroad train arrived in Oxford County on December 18, 1853. A crew of 1200 men constructed the railway through the region's unbroken wilderness. Products produced locally could now be transported in hours rather than days and at a lower cost than by horse and wagon. Cheese, agricultural machinery, wheat, hogs, milk and cattle were shipped from Ingersoll. Regular mail pickup and delivery was also provided by the railway.

An electric trolley service between Woodstock and Ingersoll operated for almost twenty-five years.

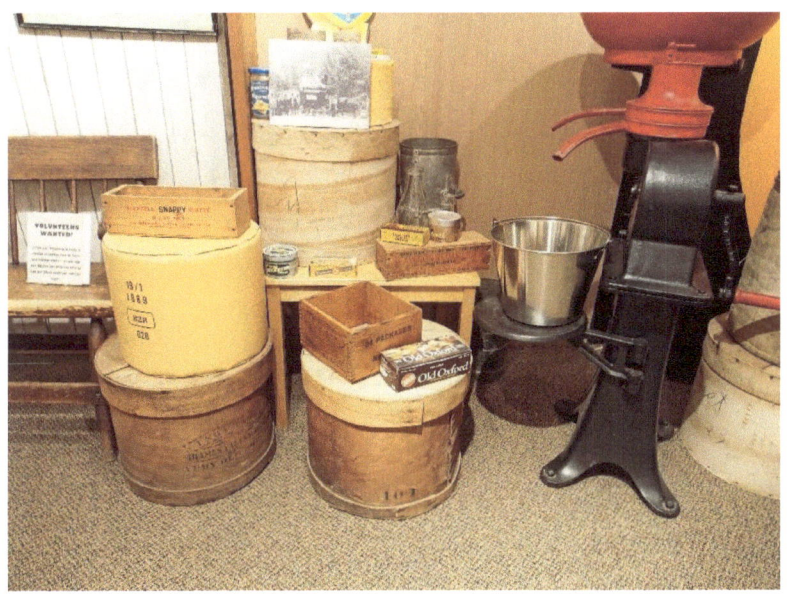

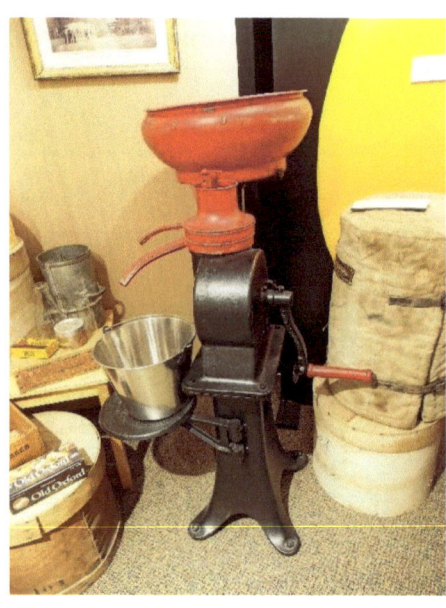

    Hiram Ranney settled in Salford in 1834. He and his wife Lydia had seven hundred acres and one hundred cows. Lydia made cheese and butter which was sold in London, Hamilton, Toronto and Brantford markets. Mrs. Ranney instructed several men in the art of cheese making. Their daughter Julia married James Harris.

    James Harris was the son of one of the original settlers of Ingersoll. Mr. Harris owned the Ingersoll Cheese Factory, the first cheese factory in the area.

    George Galloway owned the West Oxford Union Cheese Factory located east of Ingersoll near Piper's Corners. The factory became operational in time to aid in the production of curd for the Mammoth Cheese.

    Robert Facey is credited as the head cheese maker in charge of the production of the mammoth cheese. Miles Harris, Warren Schell, and James A. Crawford assisted him.

    The Mammoth Cheese was a 7,500 block of cheese created in 1866 at the James Harris Cheese Factory. It was six feet ten inches in diameter and three feet in height.

It took milk from 2,400 cows from over 250 area farms to produce the thirty-five tons of milk needed for the mammoth cheese. After being aged for three months, the block of cheese was paraded throughout the streets of Ingersoll on its way to the train station. The enormous cheese was exhibited at the State Fair in Saratoga, New York before being shipped to and showcased throughout England and Europe. The cheese was eventually bought and sold in Liverpool, England and was of excellent quality.

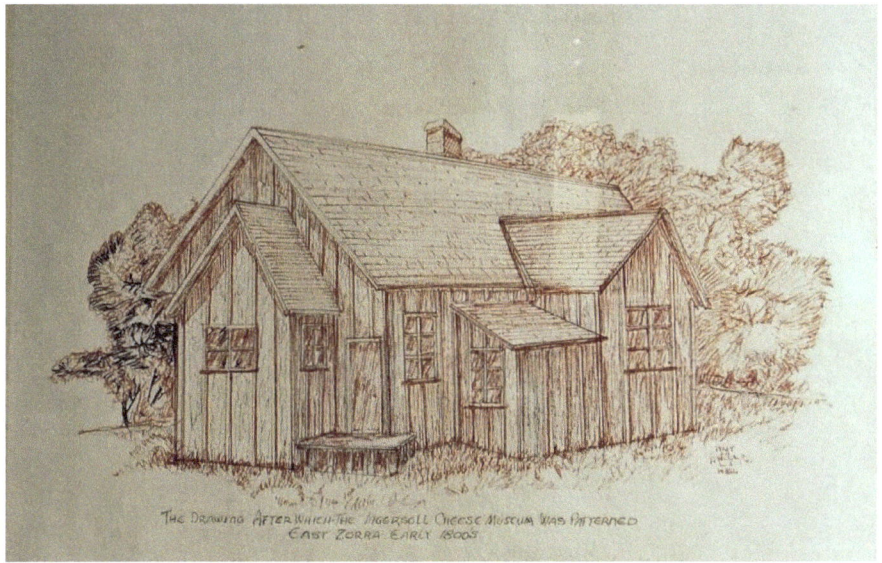

The drawing after which the Ingersoll Cheese Museum was patterned – East Zorra early 1800s

During the mid-1800s, thousands of black slaves fled from slavery on southern plantations in the United States into Canada via the Underground Railroad. With the assistance of anti-slavery supporters, 25,000-40,000 fugitives crossed into Canada between the 1830s and 1850s. Many of them settled in the areas of Windsor, Chatham, Dresden, London, Hamilton, St. Catharines, Toronto, and Otterville. The Town of Ingersoll was one of the most northerly stops along the Underground Railway and brought two hundred blacks between 1850-1851.

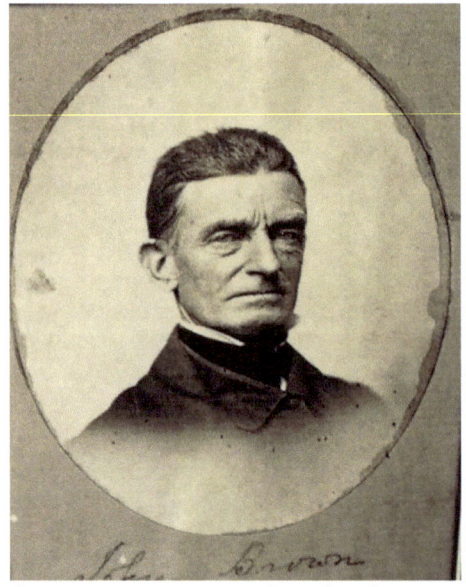

John Brown – a civil rights' activist

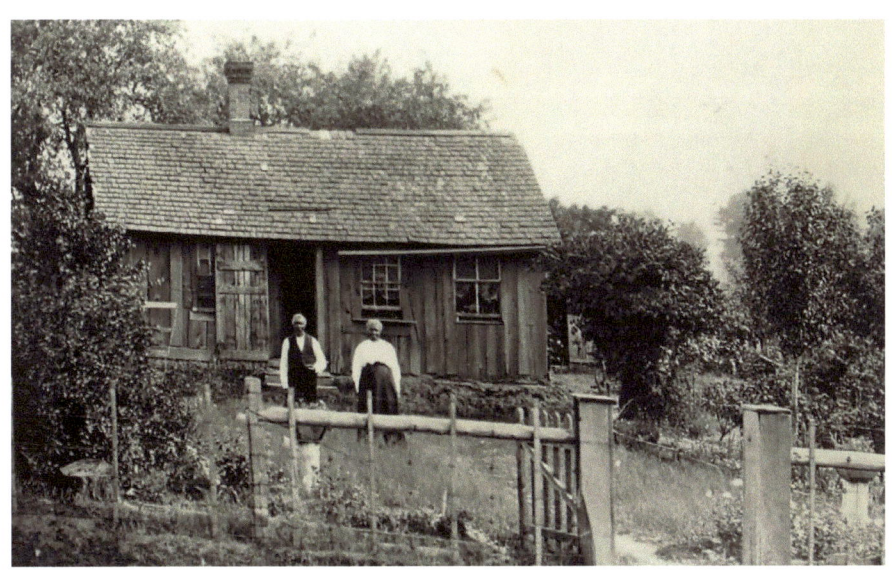

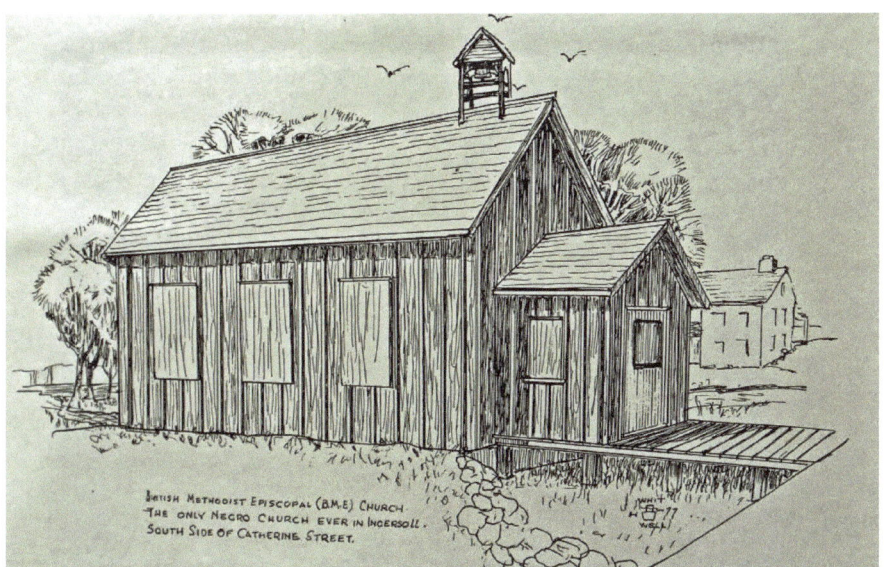

British Methodist Episcopal Church (BME) – Negro church in Ingersoll on the south side of Catherine Street

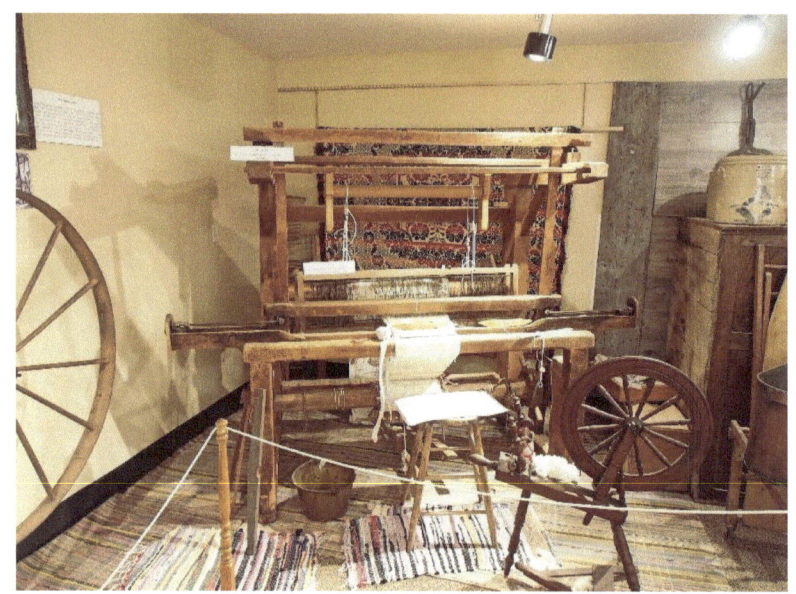

Loom

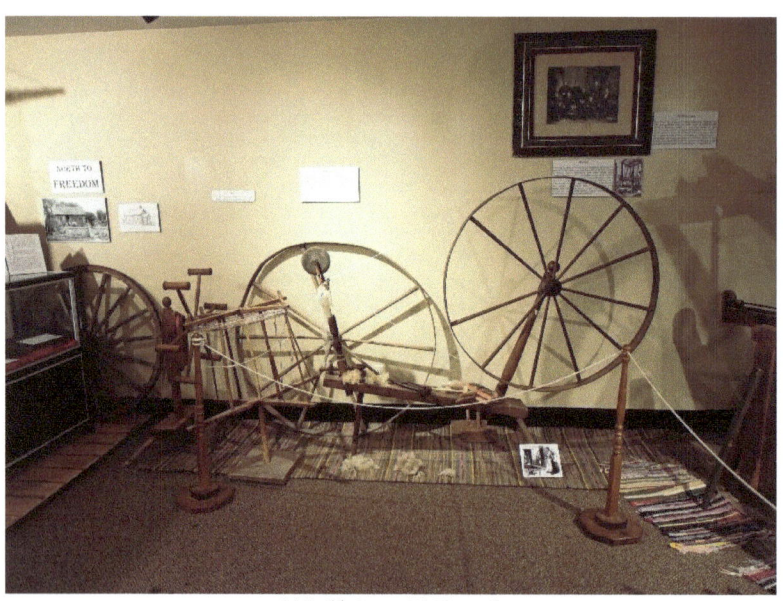

Walking Wheel

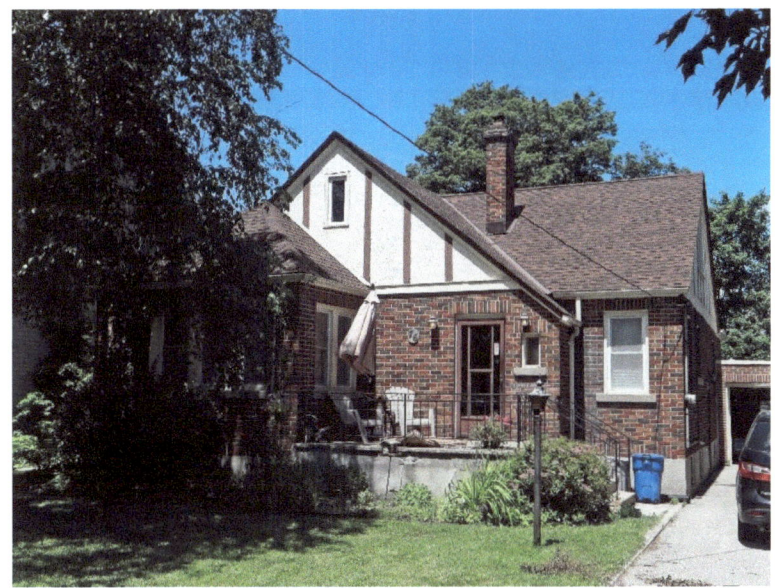

76 Duke Street

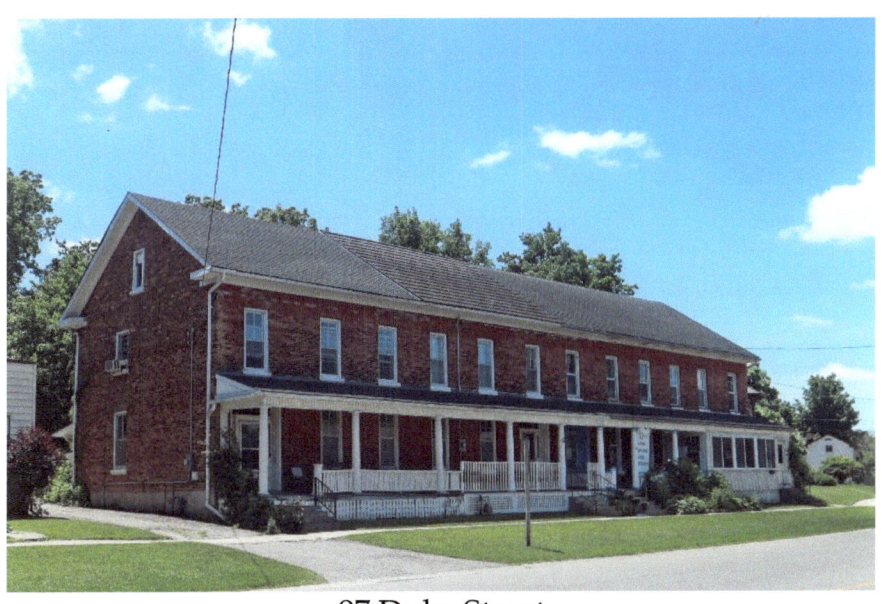

97 Duke Street

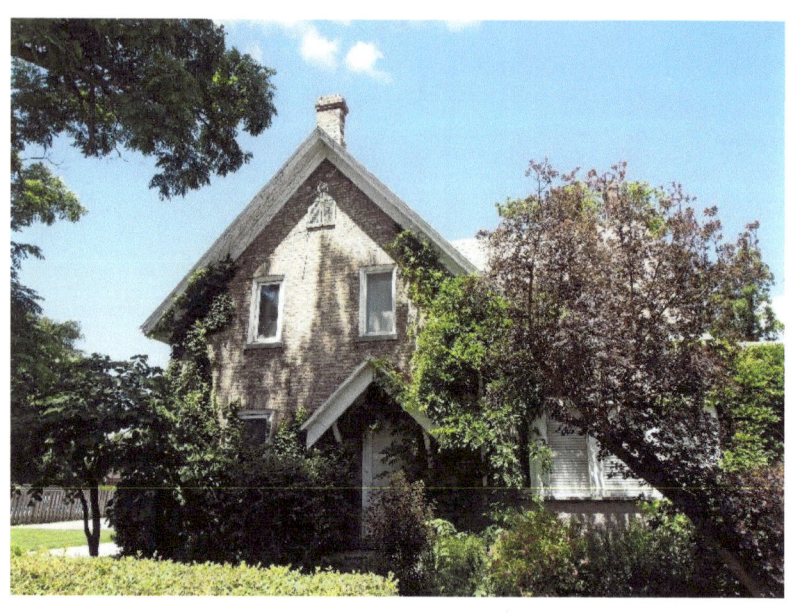

128 Duke Street – Dogwood Centre – Gothic

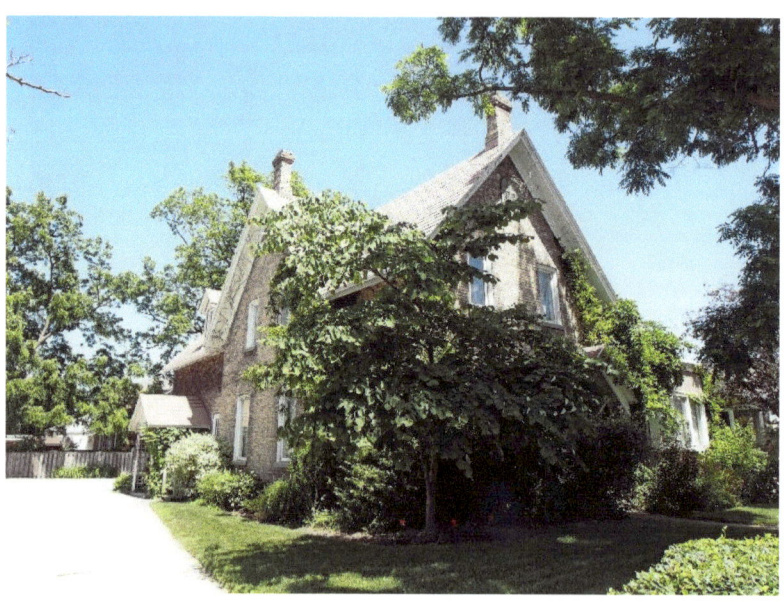

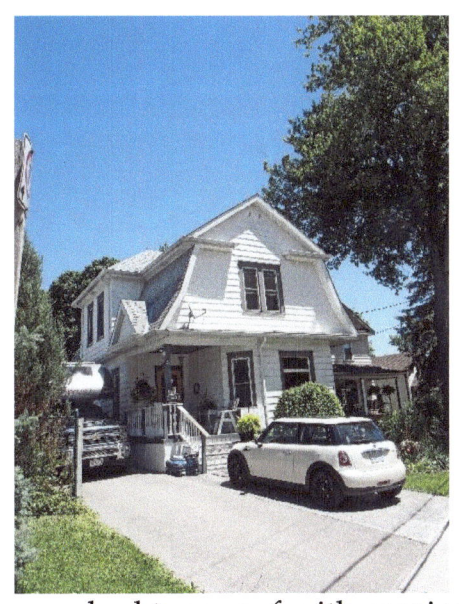

209 Hall Street – gambrel type roof with cornice return on gable

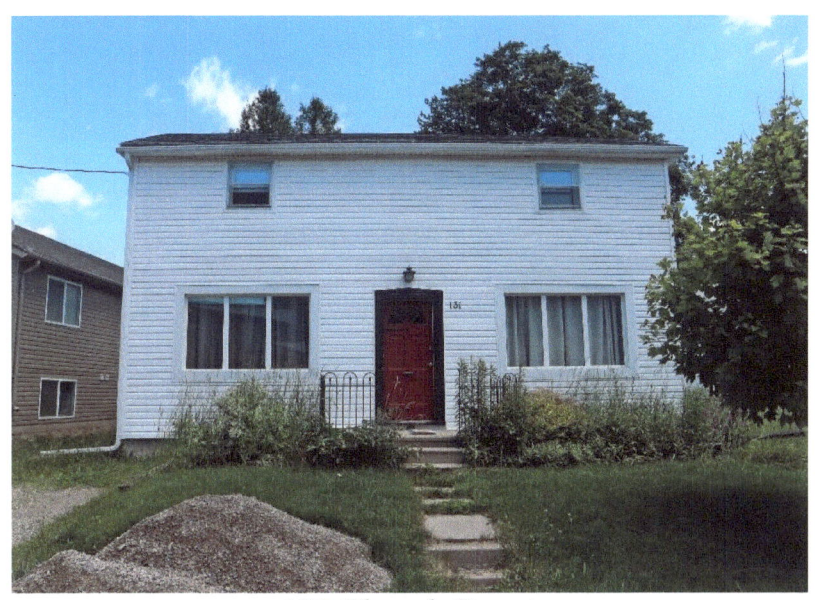

131 Church Street

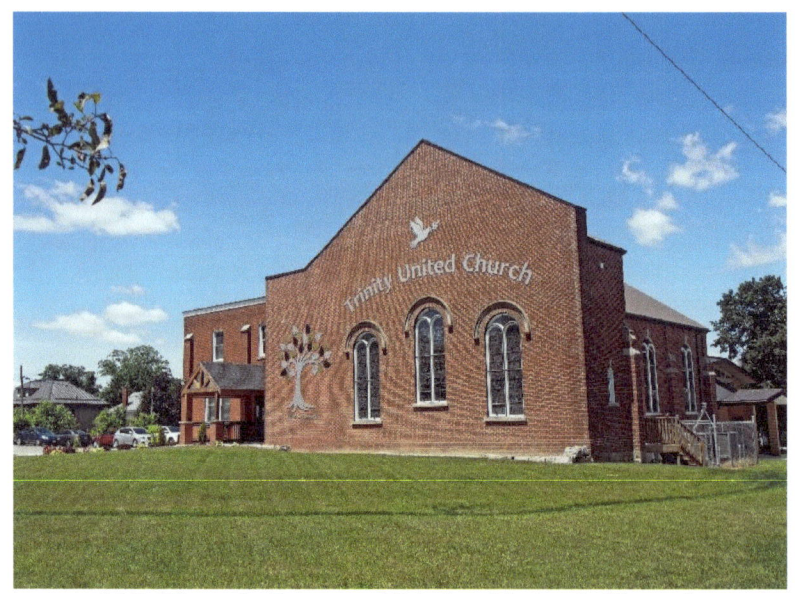

118 Church Street – Trinity United Church

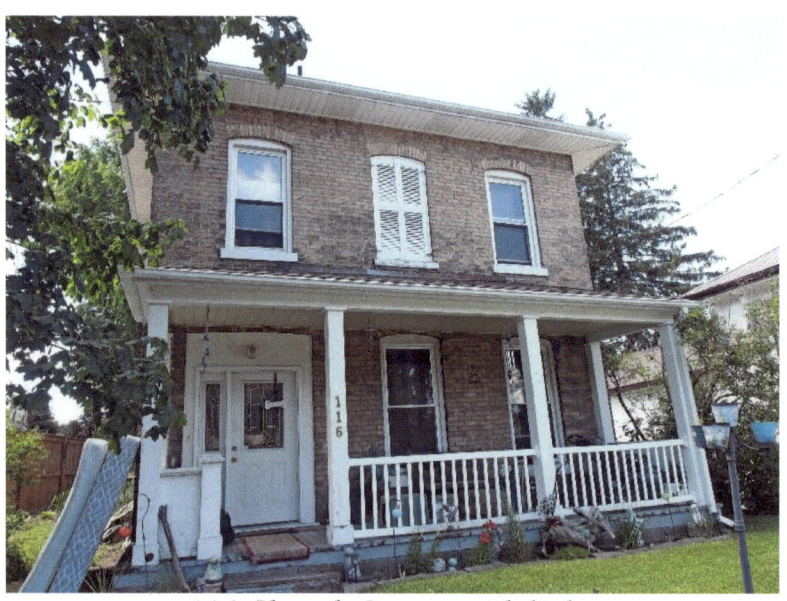

116 Church Street - sidelight

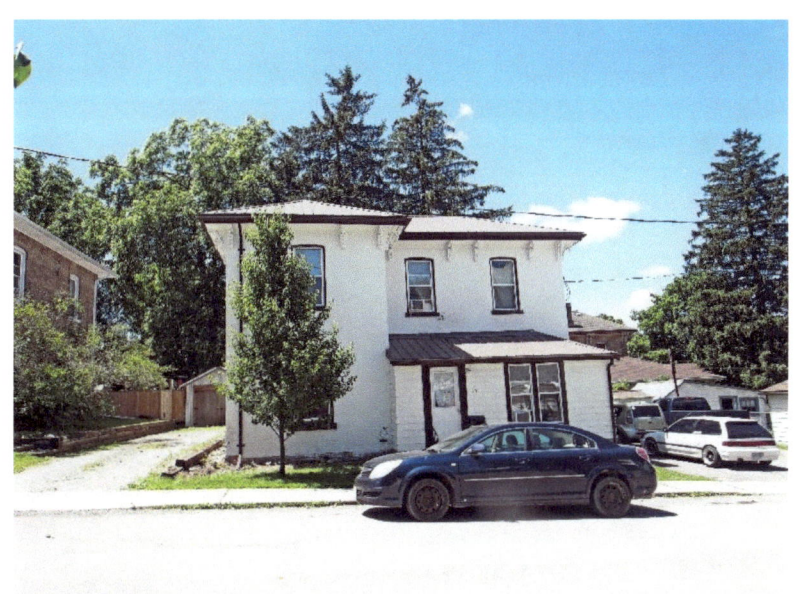

110 Church Street – hipped roof, cornice brackets

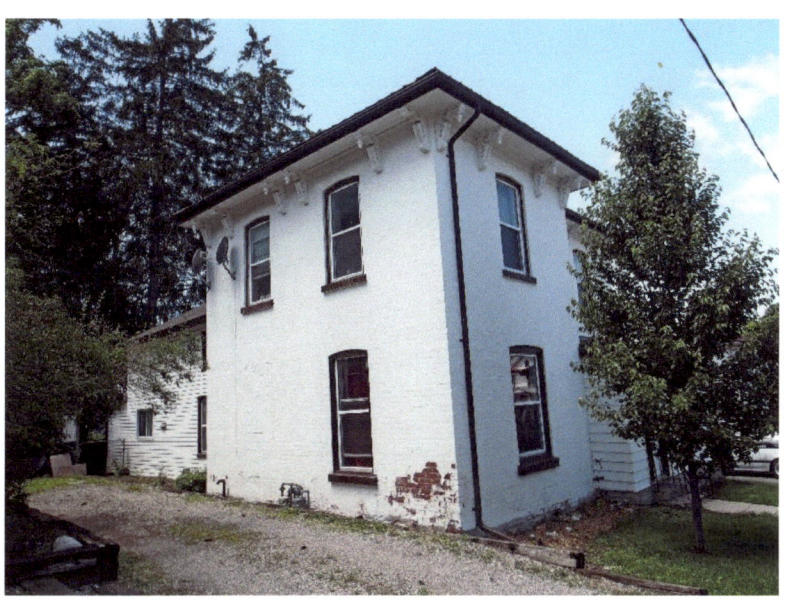

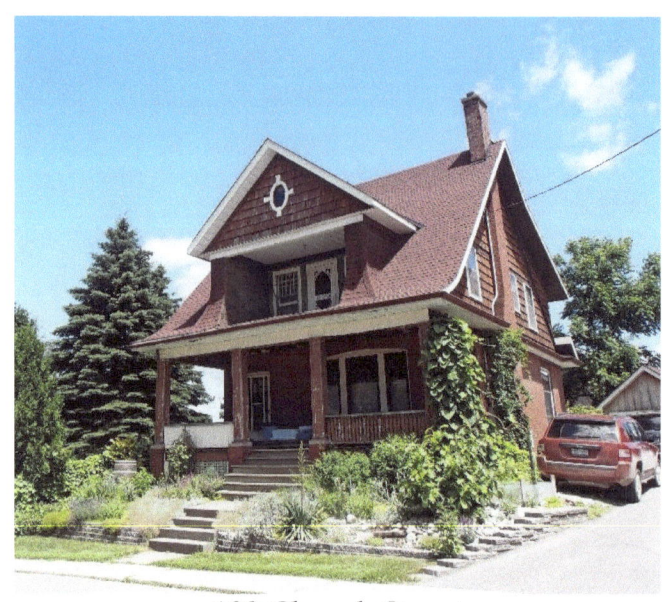

108 Church Street

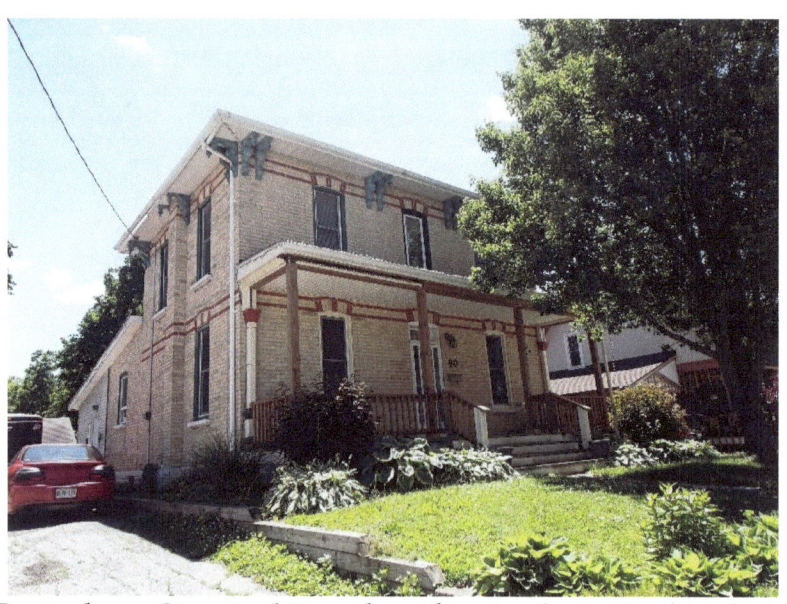

90 Canterbury Street – hipped roof, paired cornice brackets, dichromatic brickwork

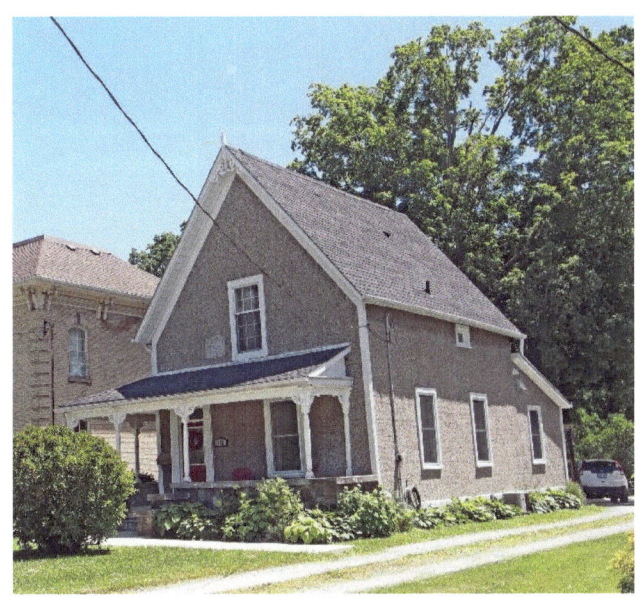

108 Canterbury Street

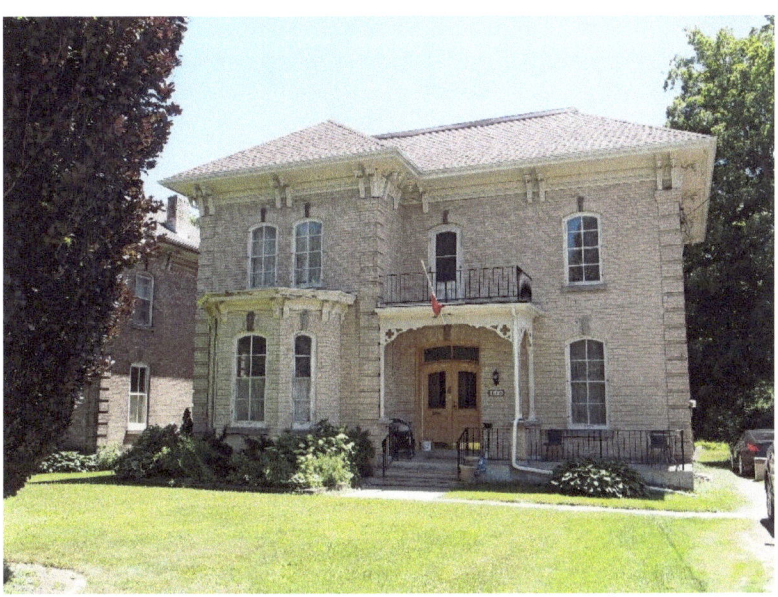

112 Canterbury Street – Italianate - hipped roof, paired cornice brackets, corner quoins, bay window, second-floor balcony, transom window above door

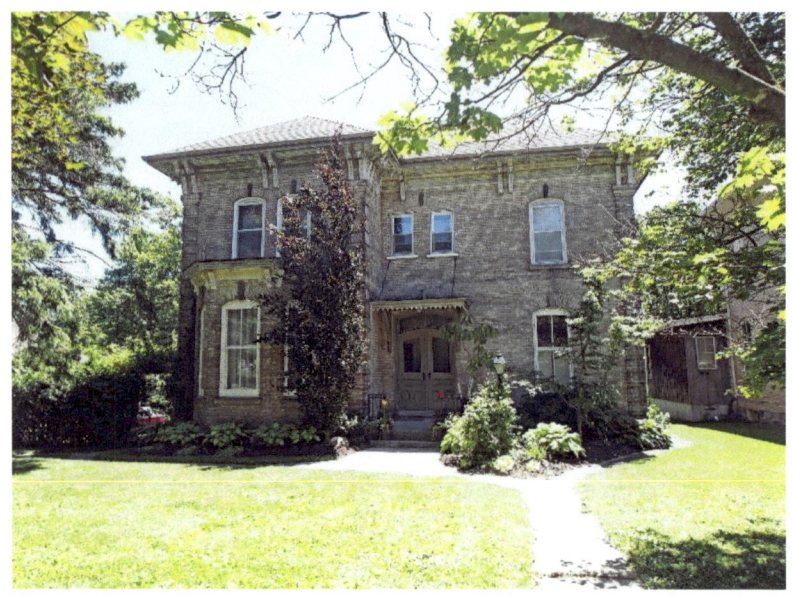

116 Canterbury Street – voussoirs and keystones, double front door with transom

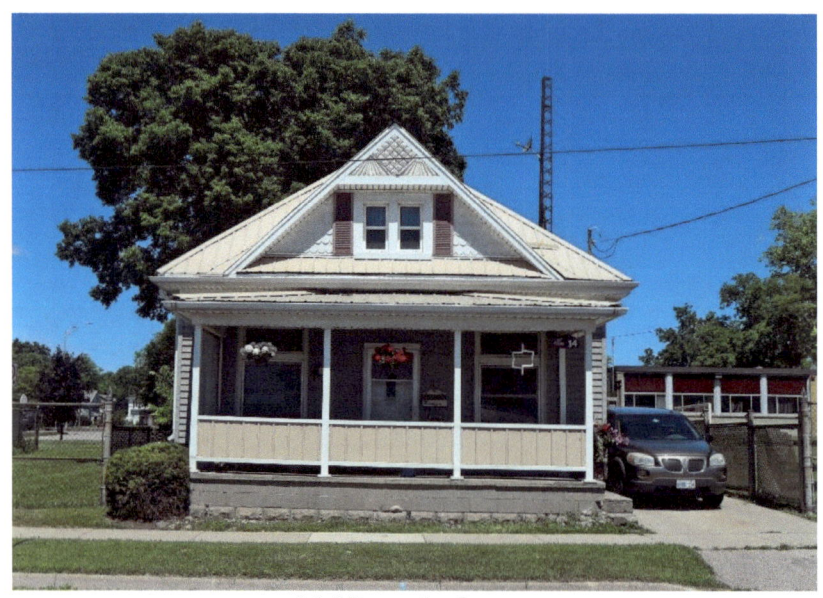

14 Victoria Street

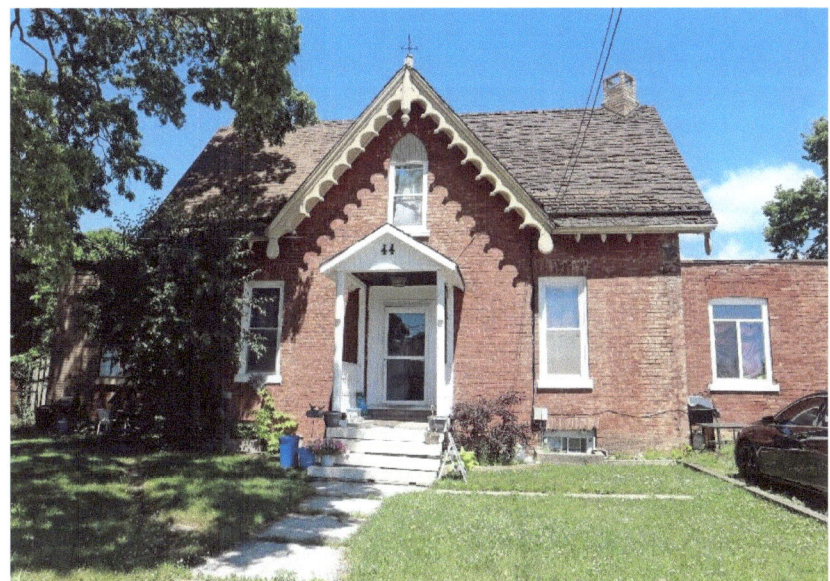

44 Victoria Street – Gothic Revival, verge board trim and finial on gable

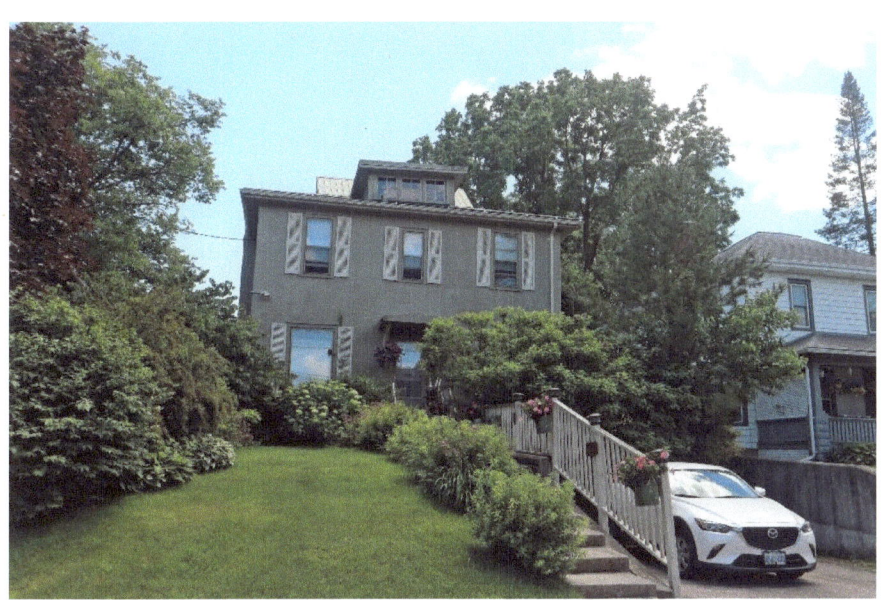

Ann Street – dormer, shutters

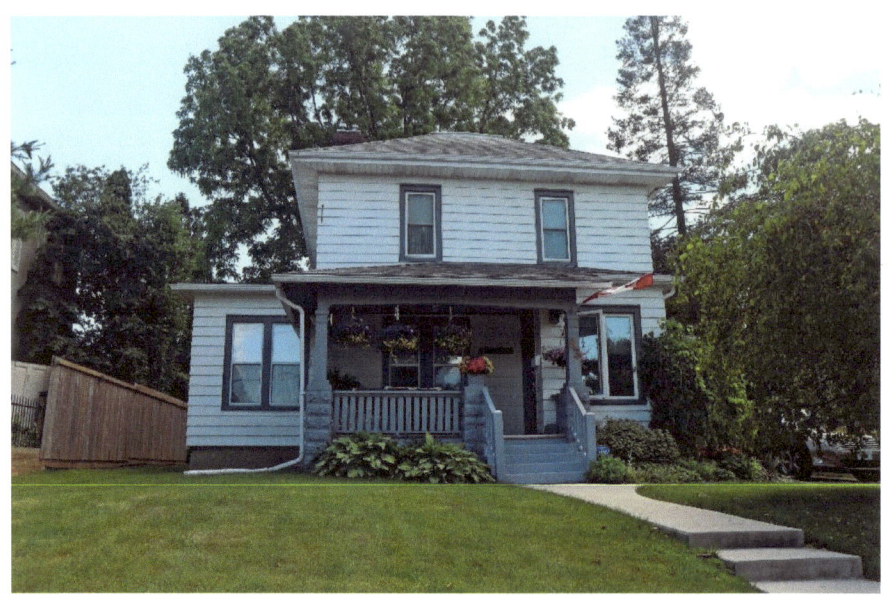
83 Ann Street – hipped roof

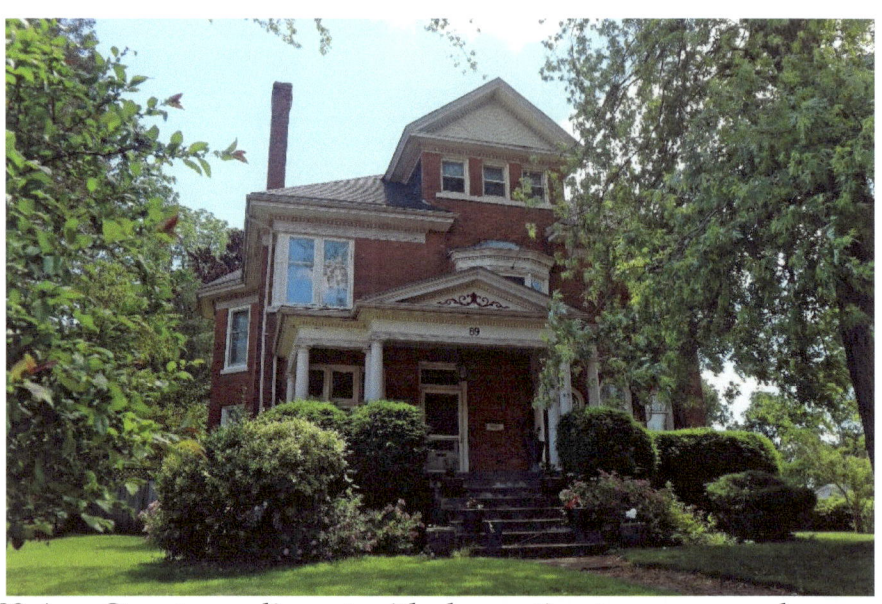
89 Ann Street – pediment with decorative tympanum, dormer with triple windows

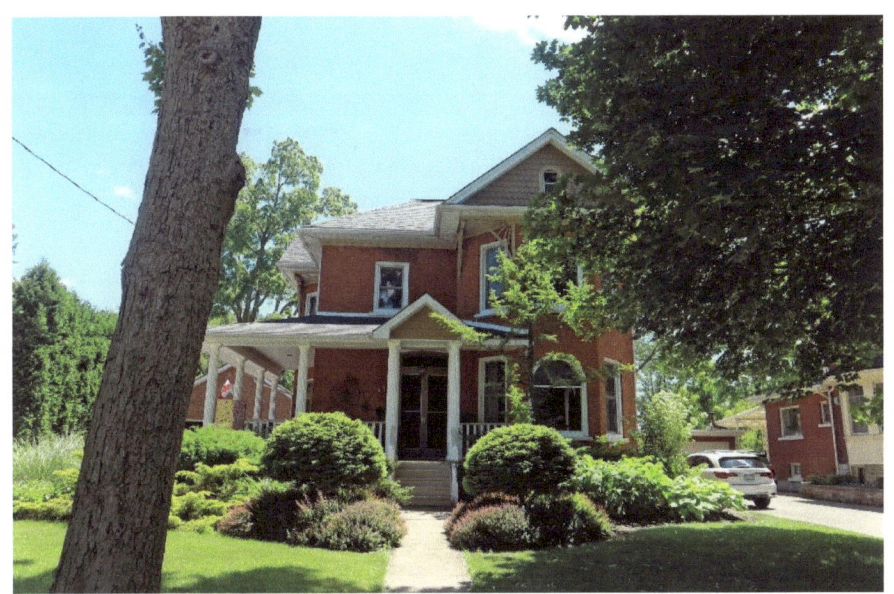

110 Ann Street – wraparound veranda

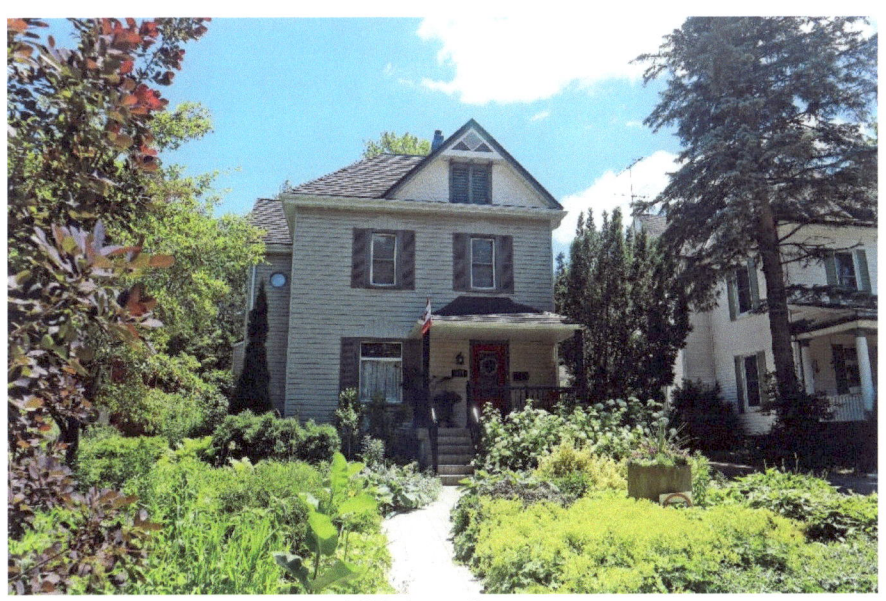

127 Ann Street

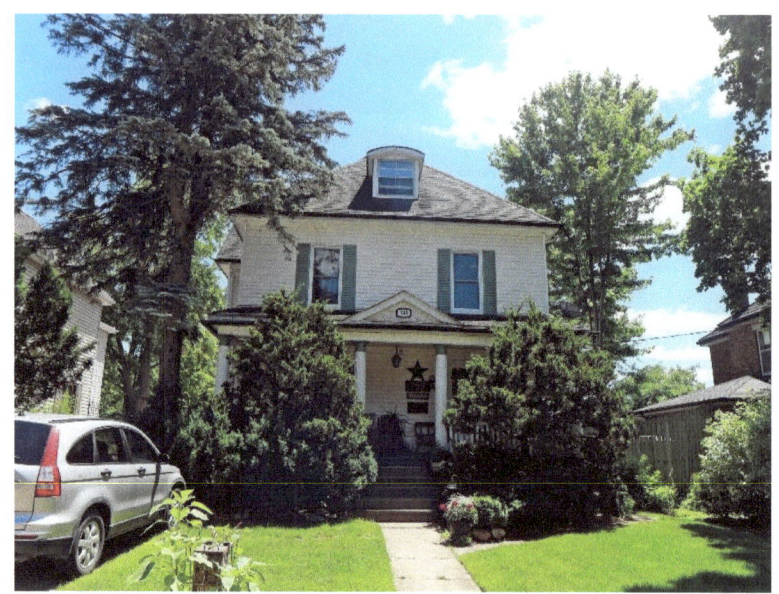
133 Ann Street – dormer in attic

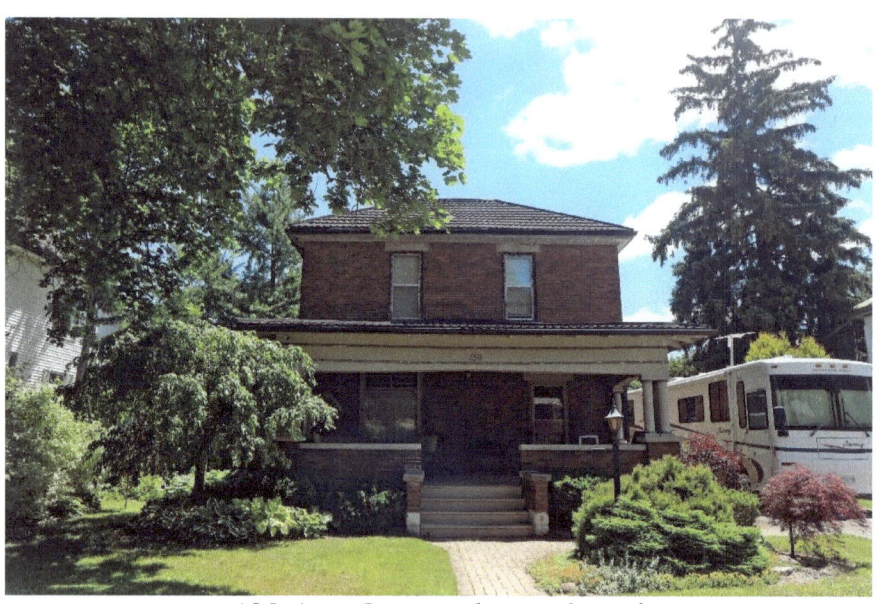
139 Ann Street – hipped roof

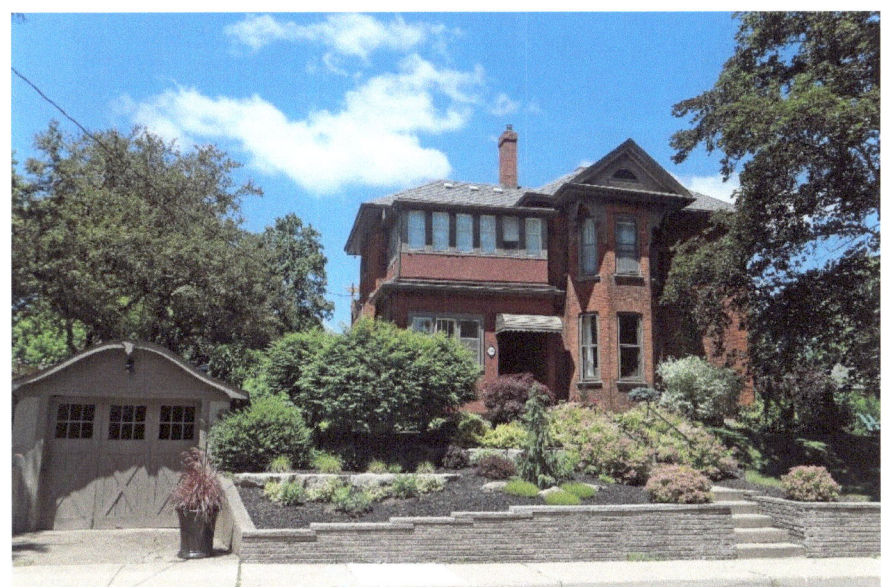

140 Ann Street – 2½-storey bay with fretwork, semi-circular window in gable, enclosed sun porch on second floor

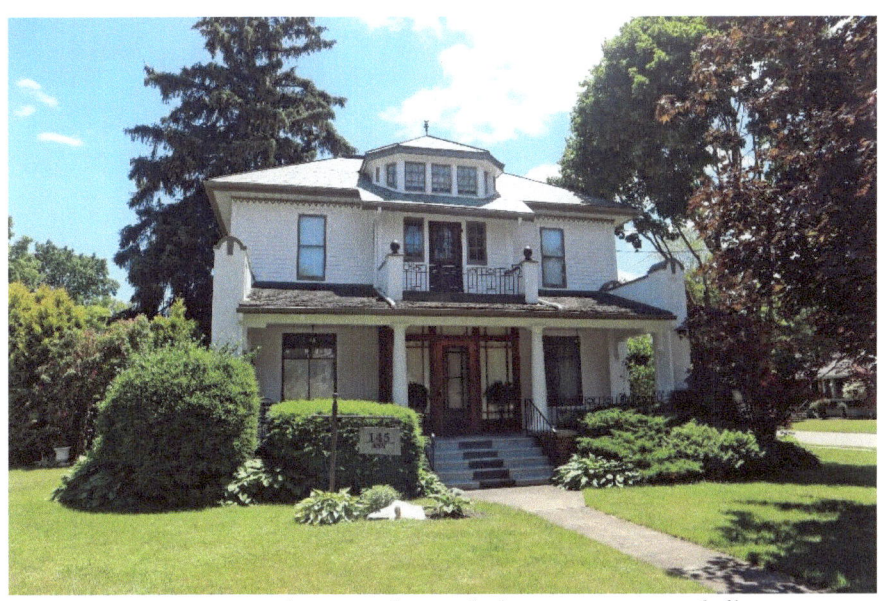

145 Ann Street – multi-windowed dormer, second-floor balcony, decorative cornice, Doric pillars supporting veranda

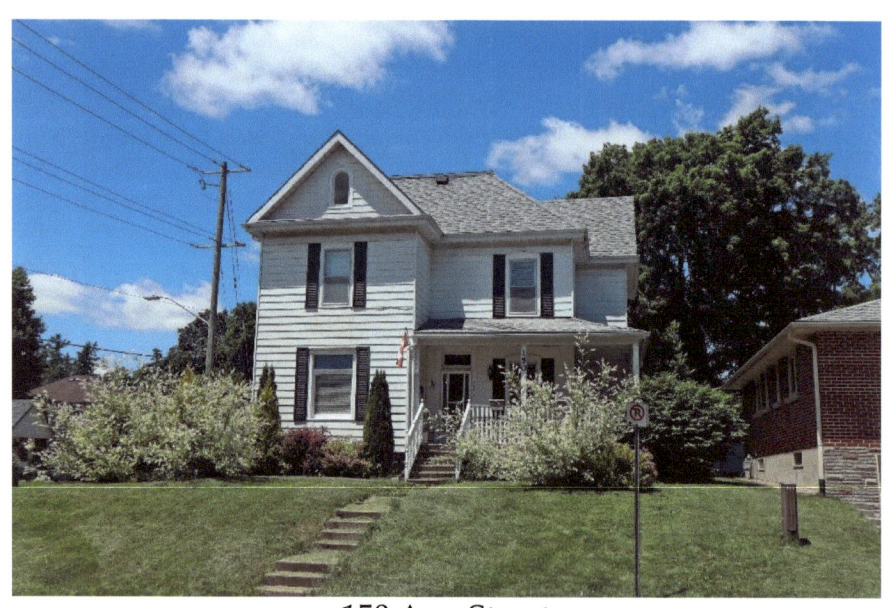

150 Ann Street

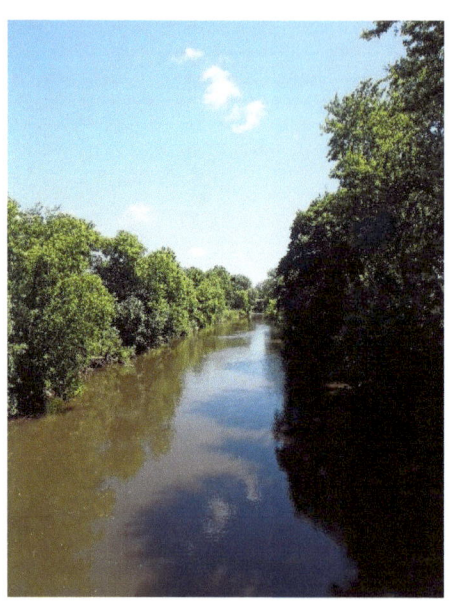

Other Books by Barbara Raue

Coins of Gold
Arrows, Indians and Love
The Life and Times of Barbara
The Cromwell Family Book
Laura Secord Discovered
Daddy Where Are You?

Montana Series
Book 1: Montana Dream
Book 2: Life on the Montana Frontier
Book 3: Montana to Boston and Back
Book 4: Montana Sons Go to War
Book 5: Montana Sons Return from War

© 2019 by Barbara Raue - All the photos in this book have been taken with my cameras. I own the rights to them.

www.ingramcontent.com/pod-product-compliance
Lightning Source LLC
Chambersburg PA
CBHW040230220526
45473CB00001B/188